JESUS, THE MIDDLE EASTERN STORYTELLER

ncient CONTEXT
Ancient FAITH

JESUS,
THE MIDDLE EASTERN STORYTELLER

ICOVER THE ANCIENT CULTURE, DISCOVER HIDDEN MEANINGS

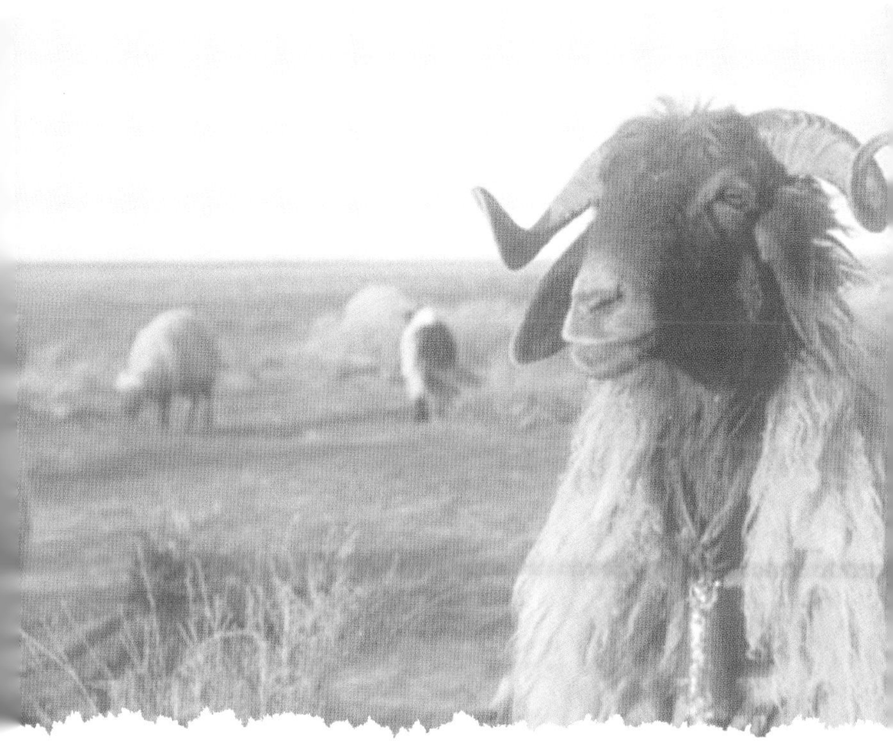

GARY M. BURGE

ZONDERVAN®

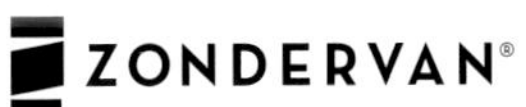

ZONDERVAN.com/
AUTHORTRACKER
follow your favorite authors

ZONDERVAN

Jesus, the Middle Eastern Storyteller

Requests for information should be addressed to:

Zondervan, *Grand Rapids, Michigan 49530*

Library of Congress Cataloging-in-Publication Data

Burge, Gary M.
Jesus, the Middle Eastern storyteller / Gary M. Burge.
p. cm. (Ancient context, ancient faith)
ISBN 978-0-310-28045-3 (softcover)
1. Jesus Christ - Parables. 2. Bible. N.T. Luke - Criticism, interpretation, etc. 3. Storytelling - Religious aspects - Christianity. 4. Middle East - Civilization. I. Title.
BT375.3.B87 2008
226.8'06 – dc22 2008021319

Interior design by Kirk DouPonce, www.DogEaredDesign.com
Maps by International Mapping

Printed in China

09 10 11 12 13 14 15 16 17 18 • 15 14 13 12 11 10 9 8 7 6 5 4 3 2 1

For Kenneth E. Bailey

Who taught me how to read a parable

Contents

Series Introduction:

Ancient Context, Ancient Faith

EVERY COMMUNITY of Christians throughout history has framed its understanding of spiritual life within the context of its own culture. Byzantine Christians living in the fifth century and Puritan Christians living over a thousand years later used the world in which they lived to work out the principles of Christian faith, life, and identity. The reflex to build house churches, monastic communities, medieval cathedrals, steeple-graced and village-centered churches, or auditoriums with theater seating will always spring from the dominant cultural forces around us.

Even the way we understand "faith in Christ" is to some degree shaped by these cultural forces. For instance, in the last three hundred years, Western Christians have abandoned seeing faith as a chiefly communal exercise (although this is not true in Africa or Asia). Among the many endowments of the European Enlightenment, individualism reigns supreme: Christian faith is a personal, private endeavor. We prefer to say, "*I have accepted Christ*," rather than define ourselves through a *community* that follows Christ. Likewise (again, thanks to the Enlightenment) we have elevated rationalism as a premier value. Among many Christians faith is a construct of the mind, an effort at knowledge gained through study, an assent to a set of theological propositions. Sometimes even knowing *what you believe* trumps belief itself.

To be sure, many Christians today are challenging these Enlightenment assumptions and are seeking to chart a new path. Nevertheless, this new path is as much a by-product of modern cultural trends than any other. For example, we live today in a highly therapeutic society. Even if we are unaware of the discipline of psychology, we are still being shaped by the values it has brought to our culture over the last hundred years. Faith today has an emotional, feeling-centered basis. Worship is measured by the emotive responses and the heart. "Felt needs" of a congregation shape many sermons.

Therefore, defining Christian faith as a personal choice based on well-informed convictions and inspired by emotionally engaging worship is a formula for spiritual formation that may be natural to us—but it may have elements that are foreign to the experience of other Christians in other cultures or other centuries. I imagine that fifth-century Christians would feel utterly lost in a modern church with its worship band and theater seating where lighting, sound, refreshments, and visual media are closely monitored. They might wonder if this *modern church* was chiefly indebted to entertainment, like a tamed, baptized version of Rome's public arenas. They might also wonder how 10,000 people can gain any sense of shared life or community when each family comes and goes by car, lives a long distance away, and barely recognizes the person sitting next to them.

The Ancient Landscape

If it is true that *every* culture provides a framework in which the spiritual life is understood, the same must be said about the ancient world. The setting of Jesus and Paul in the Roman Empire was likewise shaped by cultural forces quite different from our own. If we fail to understand these cultural forces, we will fail to understand many of the things Jesus and Paul taught.

This does not mean that the culture of the biblical world enjoys some sort of divine approval or endorsement. We do not need to imitate the biblical world in order to live a more biblical life. This was a culture that had its own preferences for dress, speech, diet, music, intellectual thought, religious expression, and personal identity. And its cultural values were no more significant than are our own. Modesty in antiquity was expressed in a way we may not understand. The arrangement of marriage partners is foreign to our world of personal dating. Even how one prays (seated or standing, arms upraised or folded, aloud or silent) has norms dictated by culture.

But if this is true—if cultural values are presupposed within every faithful community, both now and two thousand years ago—then the stories we read in the Bible may presuppose themes that are completely obscure to us. Moreover, when we read the Bible, we may misrepresent its message because we simply do not understand the cultural instincts of the first century. We live two thousand years distant; we live in the West and the ancient Middle East is not native territory for us.

Interpreting from Afar

This means we must be cautious interpreters of the Bible. We must be careful lest we presuppose that *our cultural instincts* are the same as those represented in the Bible. We must be *culturally aware* of our own place in time—and we must work to comprehend the cultural context of the Scriptures that we wish to understand. Too often interpreters have lacked cultural awareness when reading the Scriptures. We have failed to recognize the gulf that exists between who we are today and the context of the Bible. We have forgotten that we read the Bible as foreigners, as visitors who have traveled not only to a new geography but a new century. We are literary tourists who are deeply in need of a guide.

The goal of this series is to be such a guide—to explore themes from the biblical world that are often misunderstood. In what sense, for instance, did the physical geography of Israel shape its people's sense of spirituality? How did the storytelling of Jesus presuppose cultural themes now lost to us? What celebrations did Jesus know intimately (such as a child's birth, a wedding, or a burial)? What agricultural or religious festivals did he attend? How did he use common images of labor or village life or social hierarchy when he taught? Did he use humor or allude to politics? In many cases—just as in our world—the more delicate matters are handled indirectly, and it takes expert guidance to revisit their correct meaning.

In a word, this series employs *cultural anthropology, archaeology, and contextual backgrounds* to open up new vistas for the Christian reader. If the average reader suddenly sees a story or an idea in a new way, if a familiar passage is suddenly opened for new meaning and application, this effort has succeeded.

I am indebted to many experiences and people who awakened my sense of urgency about this interpretive method. My first encounter came as a student at Beirut's *Near East School of Theology* in the 1970s. Since then, scholars such as David Daube, J. D. M. Derrett, S. Safrai, M. Stern, E. P. Sanders, Charles Kraft, James Strange, Kenneth Bailey, Bruce Malina, I. Howard Marshall, and a host of others have contributed to how I read the New Testament. Bailey's many books in particular as well as his long friendship have been prominent in inspiring my efforts into the cultural anthropology of the ancient world. In addition, I have been welcomed many times by the Arabic-speaking church in Lebanon, Syria, Iraq, Jordan, Palestine, and Egypt and there became attuned to the way that cultural setting influences how we read texts. To them and their great and historic faith, I owe a considerable debt.

Finally, special thanks are due to Katya Covrett and Verlyn Verbrugge at Zondervan Publishing. Verlyn's expert editing and Katya's creativity improved the book enormously. Elizabeth Dias, my research assistant, also edited the manuscript and found weaknesses even Verlyn missed. And last (and most important), my wife, Carol, read and critiqued the manuscript during our last sabbatical in Cambridge, England. Her insight and wisdom appear in every chapter.

Soli Deo Gloria.

Gary M. Burge
Wheaton, Illinois

Chapter 1

JESUS' STORYTELLING WORLD

JESUS LIVED in a storytelling world, and he was well known for his ability as a storyteller. Throughout the Gospels Jesus is also recognized as a great teacher. The Greek term for teacher (*didaskalos*) translates the Hebrew word *rabbi* (which means "my great one," Matt. 23:8; John 1:38) and was used as an exalted title for teachers of the Jewish law in the first century. Teachers held a long and honorable history in ancient Judaism, and when Jesus began to move from village to village, particularly in Galilee, the crowds immediately recognized a skill and an authority that surpassed what they met in their synagogues. But it was his stories that everyone remembered most clearly.

JESUS AS A MIDDLE EASTERN TEACHER

When we imagine Jesus' teaching in his own time and place, we cannot use profiles of teachers from our own world to understand the nature of his work. Our culture is heir to the Greek tradition, where abstract reasoning and verbal prose are the measure of the teacher. In Jesus' world, communication involved

MOUNT OF BEATITUDES
Z. Radovan/www.BibleLandPictures.com

the use of word pictures, dramatic actions, metaphors, and stories. Rather than lecture about religious corruption, Jesus refers to the Pharisees as "whitewashed tombs." Rather than outline the failings of the temple system, he curses a fig tree.

Jesus could enter a Galilean village and within days find himself encircled by large audiences hanging on every word. It wasn't simply that he was religious or inspiring; rather, the crowds sensed that here was a skilled speaker who knew how to sound themes that were important to them. He was a man who spoke their language, who understood labor and taxes and political corruption. Here was a man who picked up the images that surrounded them every day and spun them into examples of timeless truth. Jesus had an eloquence matched to surprising wit.

Todd Bolen/www.BiblePlaces.com

A fig tree near Jerusalem

Matthew notes that when Jesus had finished his inaugural sermon in Galilee (Matt. 5–7) the audience was utterly

Todd Bolen/www.BiblePlaces.com

A first century synagogue, Gamla, Galilee

astounded, "When Jesus had finished these sayings, the crowds were amazed at his teaching" (7:28). Luke writes that when Jesus completed his first presentation in his home synagogue in Nazareth, the audience was thrilled, then stunned, then enraged; finally, they nearly killed him. Speakers know when they have successfully "landed" their message: either the audience carries you out on its shoulders with cheers and acclaim or they plot how they might toss you off a cliff (Luke 4:29).

Skilled teachers in Jesus' day could spin a good tale. They used gross exaggeration and ridiculous comparisons simply to keep their listeners with them. They used humor and puns, drama and harsh comparison in order to make their point. On one occasion Jesus criticized his opponents by telling them that their religious pursuits were absurd. They overlooked weighty spiritual matters but debated the minutia of religion as if the entire world depended on it. He told them, "You strain out a gnat but swallow a camel" (Matt. 23:24). No doubt when the crowd heard such statements, they couldn't help but laugh at the image of Pharisees picking gnats out of their teeth but swallowing entire camels. The gross comparison is both offensive and humorous—and it is clever. In Jesus' native speech (Aramaic), the word for gnat is *galma* while the

Gary M. Burge

CAMELS FROM THE SOUTHERN JORDANIAN DESERT

word for camel is *gamla*. Jesus had actually said, "You strain out a *galma* but all along you swallow *gamla*." Reversing two simple letters gave the saying a sharp-edged and memorable poignancy.

For some time, scholars have suggested that Jesus' storytelling ability was unique in his day. But this is not true. Today we have a better understanding of ancient Judaism, and it is clear that Jewish rabbis used the illustrative story with some frequency. (In the period following Jesus, we have accounts of over two thousand rabbinic stories.) Jesus—without formal training—was able to match the best of them.

Jesus lived in a world where literacy was rare and books (or scrolls) were rarer still. Scholarly brilliance was measured by the teaching skill of the rabbi, and it was often left to his students to copy down anything that might be later published. The Gospels were penned by Jesus' followers, but we have no evidence that he wrote down any of his own sayings—much less that he wrote a book. The great scholars of Jesus' day were recognized by the number of students (*talmid*) they could attract, not by the books they wrote. Communication was verbal and memorization commonplace. Thus the rabbi-scholars Johanan ben Zakkai, Gamaliel, Hillel, and Shammai did not leave their own writings behind, but rather their teachings were collected and later preserved by their followers (exactly like Jesus).

When the Gospels tell us that at one point Jesus had five thousand people sitting at his feet (Mark 6:44), it is not just to record a number; rather, it indicates the public acclaim he enjoyed. He began with twelve *talmid* (or disciples)—later we learn about seventy—and at one point five thousand and four thousand flock around him. By every first-century measure, Jesus was a respected public speaker in his day. It is no wonder that the rabbinic schools sent emissaries out to him to investigate what was going on.

The aim of the great Jewish scholar was to teach with effect. To win a crowd. To offer teachings that transformed thinking and living. One Middle Eastern proverbial saying expressed it nicely, "The great teacher never offers his students a basket of cucumbers; instead he places a peppercorn under the tongue." So many of Jesus' stories have survived in our Gospels because they are "peppercorns" that remained with his followers for years.

The Stories of Jesus

Z. Radovan/www.BibleLandPictures.com

An oil lamp from the first century

The Gospels refer to the stories of Jesus as *parables*. Parable comes from a Greek term (*parabole*) used to describe an illustrative story that creates a vibrant contrast or image for the listener. In some cases, it creates nothing more than a *word picture*: "None of you lights a lamp and puts it in a place where it will be hidden, or under a bowl. Instead you put it on its stand, so that those who come in may see the light" (Luke 11:33). In other cases it may be a narrative or story that leads the listener to a critical punch line: "The kingdom of heaven is like a merchant looking for fine pearls . . ." (Matt. 13:45).

Almost one-third of Jesus' teachings are in the form of parables. He told parables about nature (weeds in a field, Matt. 13:24–30), work and wages (the master and servant, Luke 17:7–10), even weddings and feasts (the bridesmaids, Matt. 25:1–13). This was Jesus' favorite means of teaching. He rarely spoke in general about God's quest for the lost but preferred to tell a story about a woman who had lost one of her ten silver coins and couldn't rest until she

William D. Mounce

A limestone burial box or sarcophagus from the Roman era

had found it (Luke 15:8–10). He rarely confronted the Pharisees in the abstract but preferred to think of them as "whitewashed tombs" (Matt. 23:27). Imagine the dramatic effect of this. Teachers whose outer religious life was pristine and yet whose inner spiritual motivations were dreadful reminded Jesus of Greek cemeteries where limestone tombs (called sarcophagi) on the outside were beautiful but inside were filled with dry bones.

The Skill of Jesus

But was Jesus a sophisticated teacher? Some scholars have a romantic view of him as a rural village carpenter who offered pithy and simple insights about God. Jesus earned an income as a craftsman (with wood or stone), and this was common since rabbis usually held such practical jobs. Paul, for example, was a tentmaker and the famous rabbi Shemmai was a stonemason. This is because Jewish law forbad a scholar from making money from his religious teaching. The oral laws of Judaism (the Mishnah) described the law as a "crown" worn by the teacher, but it could not be used to glorify oneself or to gain profit. This was a "worldly use of the crown" or turning the crown into a "shovel to dig with." Instead, the rabbi was to have an occupation through which God granted the means to teach

Todd Bolen/www.BiblePlaces.com

An Arab stone mason using the skills of the ancient world

(Mishnah, *Abot* 4:5). Therefore it was not only accepted, but it was expected that Jesus would have a common job.

Jesus began his public teaching ministry when he was about thirty years old (Luke 3:23) and was therefore an accomplished craftsman in his trade for a number of years. Following his early education, he probably met regularly with men who studied and debated the Jewish law over late-night communal meals. Such men called themselves *haberim* (Heb., "friends, companions") and took their mandate from Psalm 119:63, "I am a friend [*haber*] to all who fear you." The Jews at Qumran near the Dead Sea, for instance, did this regularly every night throughout the year (*Damascus Document, Geniza A*, Col 6:2–10). This means that by the age of thirty, Jesus had honed his study and debating skills for many years and was adept at theological discussions.

If the public acclaim recorded in the Gospels is any indication, Jesus was an outstanding public speaker. Crowds were impressed not only by his authority but also by his teaching skill. For instance, simplicity was one of his hallmarks. He rarely (if ever) used technical theological speech with his audiences. Rather, Jesus preferred to tell stories. But here we need a word of cultural warning: Simplicity and storytelling do not betray a lack of profundity.

The effectiveness of Jesus' work, therefore, stemmed from how he said things. And if we recognize these verbal strategies, we will not misinterpret his words. For example, Jesus (and his culture) enjoyed overstatement and gross exaggeration, but these should not be taken "literally." In Mark 9:43–47 Jesus does not want his disciples to physically mutilate themselves but wants to underscore dramatically the importance of danger of sin: "If your hand causes you to stumble, cut it off." The truest meaning of such verses will always be found in their figurative sense. He describes how we see specks in another's eye, but miss the log in our own. These are a few examples of humorous and dramatic exaggerations meant to rivet audiences.

This is perhaps where Jesus' world departs so significantly from our own. Our culture is a master of *droning prose*. Storytelling is found in film and literature, but rarely in public speech. We believe that religious speakers are effective when they can string out long arguments to defend their points, when they can persuade by the force of argument—this for us is theological sophistication. But this view betrays an important Western prejudice, that *storytelling cultures are less sophisticated than prose cultures like our own.* They are not!

Jesus' world was also filled with drama and entertainment and theater. *Jesus himself was theatrical*, and this was a feature of his teaching strategy. Rather than giving a speech about a corrupt temple, he ransacked it. When Jesus underscored the cost of discipleship, he told his disciples that they should plan to carry a cross. His culture valued the clever image, the crisp story. Jesus himself was clever and in this brilliance, people intuited his sophistication.

How Jesus' Stories Work

Jesus' best figurative stories contain a surprise. They are like a box that contains a spring—and when it is opened, the unexpected happens. They are like a trap that lures you into its world and then closes on you.

A typical example can be found in Luke 12:13–21. Rabbis were often called on to arbitrate civil disputes regarding property. On one occasion, a man's brother would not divide the inheritance. It was a squabble about the division of property.

> *And [Jesus] told them this parable. "The ground of a certain rich man yielded an abundant harvest. He thought to himself, 'What shall I do? I have no place to store my crops.'*
>
> *"Then he said, 'This is what I'll do. I will tear down my barns and build bigger ones, and there I will store my surplus grain. And I'll say to myself, "You have plenty of grain laid up for many years. Take life easy; eat, drink and be merry."' "*

In this short story Jesus sets up an assumption that was commonplace in first-century Judaism: material prosperity was a sign of God's blessing and greater accumulation was the prerogative of those who enjoyed God's good favor. At this point in the story, Jesus' audience would have been pleased, recognizing at once the privileges of the few. Then suddenly, Jesus springs the trap:

> *But God said to him, "You fool! This very night your life will be demanded from you. Then who will get what you have prepared for yourself?"*

Todd Bolen/www.BiblePlaces.com

A grain field in modern Israel

An unexpected, harrowing question is raised in a matter of seconds. The expansion of estates, the accumulation of property, the gathering of wealth *might be the quest of the fool* because at any moment, we might die. And we cannot take our estates with us. With clever storytelling, Jesus dodges the dispute and strikes at the heart of each person's motivation.

There is considerable discussion among scholars who try to give guidelines on how we should interpret the parables. The instinct to allegorize each of them down to the smallest detail has now been widely rejected. By making every element bear some meaning, we will introduce ideas into the parables that are completely foreign to them. In the last century scholars emphasized that at the heart of each parable lies a crisis—a point or points of stark contrast that shock us, forcing us to make a value judgment on a theme or character.

For instance, the rich and foolish barn builder seems to be living with God's blessing evidenced by his material wealth—until he hears God's voice, "You fool!" Suddenly we are surprised, forced to realign our thinking. And while one of the parables does have allegorical elements (the parable of the sower), still, this is secondary to the crisis of decision that the hearer experiences when the parable is heard correctly.

David Bivin/www.LifeintheHolyLand.com

A squad of Israeli soldiers

One of the parables most commonly subject to abuse is the parable of the good Samaritan. Christians have regularly sought meaning in each element of the story. The wounded man means one thing, the donkey of the Samaritan another, the inn that gives him aid still another. I was discussing this problem with a Middle Eastern Christian once and he told me that we in the West have utterly lost the meaning of the story. So, in Jerusalem one afternoon he told me his own version of it:

Not long ago in Jerusalem's famed Hadassah Hospital, an Israeli soldier lay dying. He had contracted AIDS as a result of his gay lifestyle and was now in the last stages of the disease's terrible course. His father was a famous Jerusalem rabbi, and both he and the rest of his family had disowned him. He was condemned to die in his shame. The nursing staff on his floor knew his story and carefully avoided his room. Everyone was simply waiting for his life to expire.

The soldier happened to be part of a regiment that patrolled the Occupied West Bank, and his unit was known for its ferocity and war-fighting skills. The Palestinians living in occupation hated these troops. They were merciless and could be cruel. Their green berets always gave them away.

One evening the soldier went into cardiac arrest. All the usual alarms went off, but the nursing staff did not respond. Even the doctors looked the other way. Yet on the floor another man was at work—a Palestinian Christian janitor—who knew this story as well and also knew the meaning of the emergency. *Incredibly, he was a man whose village had been attacked by this soldier's unit.* When the Palestinian heard the alarm and witnessed the neglect, his heart was filled with compassion. He dropped his broom, entered the soldier's room, and attempted to resuscitate the man by giving him cardiopulmonary resuscitation. The scene was remarkable: a poor Palestinian man, a victim of this soldier's violence, now tried to save his enemy while those who should have been doing this stood on the sidelines.

My Arab Christian friend told me: when you understand *this story*, you will understand the parable of the good Samaritan. When you understand what it means for an enemy to love an enemy—and for the righteous to show neglect—then you will have a picture of the power of God's grace at work in a person's heart.

Pursuing the Cultural Keys

Perhaps the most important issue is for us to understand the cultural elements at work in each parable. These are stories told from another culture and time, and we read them as foreigners. What does it mean when a young son asks for his inheritance? Or when a coin is lost? The parables are like music being played out with rhythms from another world. And if we cannot recognize this music—or worse yet, if we fail even to admit our own

JACK GUEZ/Staff/Getty Images

Hadassah Hospital, Jerusalem

foreignness to its sounds—we will miss their deeper meanings and misrepresent what Jesus intended to teach.

A parable is like a political cartoon in modern culture. Its images may be exaggerated (e.g., Bill Clinton's nose, George Bush's ears), its elements distorted, and its punch line unmistakable *to those who understand its context.* In every society effective communication exploits predictable attitudes and responses. Irony, humor, and pain are conveyed when these values are broken. But if you cannot read the values, you cannot see the punch line.

In a Jewish book called Ben Sirach we are told that a nobleman is known by "the way he walks" (Sir. 19:30). Sirach assumes that we understand what such "noble walking" looks like and fails to tell us. It is left to us to unlock the cultural assumptions behind the statement, and then we learn that in this society distinguished men do not run but walk and that the slower they walk, the more honorable they are. (Architecturally the Jerusalem temple even reinforced this with *irregular steps* built into its southern porches, steps that force a worshiper to slow down.) As we will see, in the parable of the prodigal son, this one insight will mean everything.

In Luke 9:59–62 Jesus responds to a would-be disciple by telling the man to come and follow him.

> *But [the man] replied, "Lord, first let me go and bury my father."*
> *Jesus said to him, "Let the dead bury their own dead, but you go and proclaim the kingdom of God."*
> *Still another said, "I will follow you, Lord; but first let me go back and say good-by to my family."*
> *Jesus replied, "No one who puts a hand to the plow and looks back is fit for service in the kingdom of God."*

These are odd responses by any measure. A *literal* reading implies that Jesus would not even permit these men to bid farewell to their families or to take up the responsibility of burying a parent. Then we learn that the literal reading has betrayed us, for in Jesus' culture one avoids sounding offensive by avoiding direct denials. (We might do this as well. "Come to our home for dinner Friday." "Thank you for asking, but let me check with my wife." Code: I really don't wish to come, but I cannot tell you directly.)

Todd Bolen/www.BiblePlaces.com

The south entry steps to the ancient Jerusalem Temple

Both of these men are offering manufactured excuses that preserve their honor while all along denying Jesus. To "say farewell" is an attempt to appeal to family duty and so shirk Jesus' call. To "bury one's father" actually means that the man is appealing to his duty to remain at home until his father dies (is buried) so that he can then make decisions for himself. *The Middle East for centuries has been a world that shelters honor by permitting the manufacture of excuses.* Jesus knows it—and every ancient reader of the gospel knew it. And in this case Jesus is denying its use.

Three Interpretative Steps

As we listen to most of Jesus' stories, we notice three steps that will guide our study. First, as listeners we are drawn into the familiar and sometimes arresting images in the story. They are a part of the ancient world, and a listener who lived in that world would enjoy them immensely. But it is their familiarity that pulls us into the story. Once Jesus began with this opening line: "In a certain town there was a judge who neither feared God nor cared what people thought. And there was a widow in that town who kept coming to him with the plea, 'Grant me justice against my adversary' " (Luke 18:2–3).

The drama has been set, the characters have been introduced, and the ancient courtroom with its bribes and noise are before us. *To think of a modern court is to utterly misunderstand the story.*

Second, the drama of the story begins to press us, and we intuit that we will be forced to make a decision, to experience a crisis, to confront a problem. In another story, Jesus told about a poor man who was a tenant farmer plowing another person's field. But one day while his plow was cutting a furrow, his blade struck a buried box of treasure. *Now what should he do?* He cannot steal it by carrying it away, nor could he imagine handing it over to the field's owner.

In the ancient world treasure was hidden in time of conquest or threat of robbery—and ancient treasures belonged to no one. (In 1998 at the excavation of Dor, Israel, two hundred pounds of silver were found in a pot in the floor of a home!) So to test the treasure's ownership, the man makes a decision: he will rebury the treasure, sell all he has, and offer to buy the field. If the field's owner knew the treasure was there and owned it he would never sell—but he sells because it isn't his money (Matt. 13:44).

Third, the story forces us to reflect on the crisis we have just

Z. Radovan/www.BibleLandPictures.com

SILVER COINS FROM THE DOR EXCAVATION, ISRAEL

witnessed. We do not decode the elements of the story looking for meaning; we instead concentrate on the crisis and reflect on its many meanings. When a shepherd looks diligently for one lost sheep and finds it only to return home to a village celebration, *what does it mean* to know a searching God that cares that profoundly for any who are lost?

Jesus' skill as a storyteller was well established as his ministry in Galilee matured. But to hear them as his first audience heard them will be like plowing a field we know well — only to discover treasures we never knew existed.

Chapter 2

The Friend Who Came at Midnight

Luke 11:1–13

WHAT EMPOWERS and inspires prayer? The answer to this question betrays our instincts about spiritual life at their most fundamental level. Our focus can either be on *our activity* as we pray or it can be on *God's character* as we pray. When prayer is successful, is our instinct to look for *what we did right* and then try to duplicate it? This brings us around to a basic spiritual question: Is prayer about method — or is it about God? No doubt the answer to this question will shape everything about us.

Jesus' first-century world was no stranger to these questions. It is clear that his followers believed that in him they had found a man for whom prayer was unique. He was confident when he prayed; he spoke to God in a manner that seemed unusually personal and intimate.

Lord, Teach Us to Pray

In Luke 11 Jesus has just completed a time of prayer. The chapter begins by providing some insight into *how* he prayed. He prayed privately and yet his disciples were with him. Luke 9:18 gives the same impression: "Once when Jesus was praying in

---

Byzantine villa
Todd Bolen/www.BiblePlaces.com

private and his disciples were with him, he asked them, 'Who do the crowds say I am?' " Privacy was not viewed in the same manner in Jesus' world. One could be "praying alone" and yet have people nearby.

Library of Congress, LC-matpc-04800/www.LifeintheHolyLand.com

Jews praying at the Western/Wailing Wall in the 19th century, Jerusalem

When the disciples ask Jesus to teach them to pray, we are struck with how odd the question seems. These men are Jews. They know how to pray. Prayer has been a part of their lives since childhood. Yet here they intuit that Jesus has something they do not. He has access to God in prayer that they covet.

Many scholars believe that two characteristics typified prayer in first-century Judaism. First, prayer was formal and (what we might call) liturgical. Because of the dignity and holiness of God, prayer might be the recitation of Scripture (the Psalms perhaps) or set sayings.

Second, prayer was likely spoken in Hebrew, the language of the Torah, which in Jesus' day was not a language spoken by the common person. The language of the street was Aramaic, another Semitic language related to Hebrew and acquired by Israel during its Babylonian exile. Therefore, regular prayer would have been highly stylized, following a language that was awkward to the average person.

Jesus likely stood out in two respects: he prayed in Aramaic and he prayed casually, even conversationally. His prayers do not reflect any of the set forms of his day (no blessing of the nation, land, or temple); they are instead expressions of personal concern. For example, in Matthew 6:7 he is critical of prayers that are filled with "babbling" and instead urges that prayer be heartfelt, private, and sincere because God will particularly hear all *secret prayers* uttered with honesty. This is the moment when Jesus gives his followers a sample of how prayer ought to sound—what we know as the Lord's Prayer (Matt. 6:9–13).

In Luke 11:2–4 we find a shortened version of this prayer. The Lord's Prayer is a model prayer that reflects the concerns that need to appear in prayers, and most scholars agree that Jesus no doubt taught it in Aramaic. The opening word "Father" (11:2) reflects the Aramaic word "Abba," and this was so well known as Jesus' habit in prayer that it became a liturgical form used in Greek-speaking churches in Paul's day (Rom. 8:15; Gal. 4:6).

Most discussions of prayer end with Jesus' model prayer. However, this is not where Jesus' explanation ends. After he provides this model prayer, he continues with a story that embodies all of the primary values Jesus sees at work in prayer. And this is the story we have come to hear.

The Friend Who Comes at Midnight

Jesus begins by setting up a scene known to every person who lived in a rural Galilean village. Such villages with as few as a thousand people were scattered throughout Galilee. Cana, Bethsaida, Magdala, Nazareth, and Capernaum are a few of these mentioned in the New Testament. In his first-century life

Todd Bolen/www.BiblePlaces.com

The first century mountain-top village of Gamla, Galilee

story, the Jewish historian Josephus says that there were about two hundred such villages in Galilee at this time, though this is surely exaggerated. He refers specifically to about forty villages with names such as Gamla and Yodefat.

Jesus begins his story with two scenes: one scene that *will never happen* and another scene that will. The key is for us to understand the cultural features presumed in each part of the story and apply it to prayer.

What will not happen? Jesus first sets up a paragraph that outlines an unimaginable scenario:

> *Suppose you have a friend, and you go to him at midnight and say, "Friend, lend me three loaves of bread; a friend of mine on a journey has come to me, and I have nothing to set before him." And suppose the one inside answers, "Don't bother me. The door is already locked, and my children and I are in bed. I can't get up and give you anything."*

This scene would not be uncommon to village life in the first century. While travel at night was unusual in village culture in Galilee, when an unexpected guest arrived the first obligation of the host was to present the visitor with food—*and food must always be served with newly baked bread.*

It is not true that the host has "nothing" to set out. He has something—but it is not enough, not good enough, not appropriate for guests. Bread is central to every meal and serves as the fork and spoon of eating from common dishes. To serve stale bread or no bread at all would be shameful and unimaginable. No host would even consider it.

But at stake here is not simply the honoring of the traveler or the honor of the surprised host. At stake is the honor of the entire village. In this world, life is lived *corporately*, and honor is a value held not simply by the individual but by the community. Therefore, the problem of hosting a meal at midnight is a *village problem*, not merely a personal problem. Village members each share the responsibility of upholding the village reputation. Many residents are likely related (with multiple levels of cousins intermarrying). Therefore *family honor* and *village honor* likely overlap significantly.

But a solution is at hand. Most poorer villages had communal ovens that were shared and rotated. Every oven, even private ones, were kept outside the home. Therefore the host knows who has baked that day—he knows where fresh bread may be located and whom he may ask. Above all, one thing is on

Z. Radovan/www.BibleLandPictures.com

BREAD FROM THE MIDDLE EAST

Todd Bolen/www.BiblePlaces.com. Used by permission of Nazareth Village. www.nazarethvillage.com

A FIRST CENTURY KITCHEN RECONSTRUCTED IN NAZARETH

Todd Bolen/www.BiblePlaces.com. Used by permission of Nazareth Village. www.nazarethvillage.com

AN ARAB MAKING BREAD OVER AN OPEN FIRE

David Bivin/www.LifeintheHolyLand.com

A Bedouin tent in the wilderness

his mind: he must call together all resources in order to bring honor to his community and to this guest. Everyone would understand—everyone would respect his concern. *Poor communities must share their resources in order to meet unexpected needs.*

I have observed this tradition in many countries in the Middle East. Recently I was traveling through Cairo, Egypt, and decided to visit a little girl my wife and I support through World Vision, a Christian relief agency. I was taken across the city by taxi with a World Vision staff person, and when we reached our destination neighborhood, we walked through incredible scenes of poverty. When we came to our apartment block, we ascended stairs till we reached the fifth floor, where we were greeted by a proud father and his family. His little daughter was dressed beautifully and waiting for us, and we exchanged greetings and small gifts.

Then the father appeared from around the corner carrying a *case of genuine Coca-Cola* in glass bottles. He was proud and smiling and he offered me one first. I happen to dislike Coke enormously, but my staff escort whispered in my ear in English that I was obliged to drink not one but perhaps three. And I did.

When we left, I asked about the Coke. And I noticed that as we descended the stairs families throughout the building were watching us and waving. I learned something that humbled me. The case of Coke was worth so much money that the *entire building* had put its money together in order to honor me with the best refreshment money could buy. I was the first Westerner to come to the building—and everyone's honor was on the line. In order to honor me properly, seven families had to share what little they had.

Luke 11:5 tells us that this host is a "friend" to his neighbors. He is an honorable man standing in good relation to the village. Therefore he goes to a neighbor to present his dilemma—*and he knows that the neighbor will respond.* The neighbor will share because his is a village that honors visitors.

Now Jesus wonders: Can anyone imagine the neighbor whispering from his door, "Leave me alone. I am asleep with my children and I cannot help you"? This is shocking—and unimaginable. Peasant homes were often one small room with an elevated "porch" near the back (we have excavated these throughout Israel). The entire family would commonly sleep together on this porch while their possessions and animals might be found in the front half of the dwelling. Now Jesus' question remains: Would sleeping with your children be a sufficient excuse to deny such a request? Would a good neighbor refuse to support the reputation of the village and the needs of his friend? *Of course not!* He would awaken his children and the entire household and use this as an opportunity to demonstrate the importance of hospitality.

Todd Bolen/www.BiblePlaces.com

THE "SIQ"—THE MAIN ENTRANCE—INTO PETRA, JORDAN

When I was younger, I remember traveling through southern Jordan with a friend when we decided to camp overnight in the valleys of the ancient stone city of Petra. We hitchhiked to Ma'an and then caught another ride west to those valleys made famous by an Indiana Jones movie. That night we laid out our sleeping bags in one of Petra's two thousand-year-old caves and found the entire experience, well, frightening. Too dark. Too quiet. Too wild. But in the distance we saw the campfires of the nomadic Bedouin. Families with their sheep and goats were settled down throughout the area.

We decided they'd like a surprise visit. And surprise them we did: emerging from the deep darkness of the night, two foreigners stumbled to get out rough greetings in Arabic. But it was the next moment I remember so well. Everyone around the fire jumped up; a young baby lying on an Arab rug was immediately moved to some grass, the rug was shaken out, and it was laid out before us as seating.

Then a man unsheathed a knife and began carving what must have been a leg of a lamb that was in a kettle hanging over the fire. And there we sat—the baby lying in the bushes while we ate Bedouin lamb on the community's best rug in the middle of the night. It was all smiles and laughter and handshakes—and the trading of simple gifts. It was Middle East hospitality and honoring tied to a tradition that was as old as Jesus' story.

What will happen? Luke 11:8 now turns the story on its head and brings us to Jesus' insight concerning prayer. "I tell you" is Jesus' verbal tip to his listeners. Here comes the surprise:

> *I tell you, though he will not get up and give him anything because he is his friend, yet because of his anaideia he will rise and give him whatever he needs. (personal trans.)*

Jesus now reminds his audience what will inspire the neighbor to arise, wake his children, and provide fresh bread to the surprised host. He will *not* supply bread because of "friendship." The neighbor does not lie in bed and tell himself, "Well, since this is my friend and I like him, I believe I will give him what he wants." Indeed, they are friends (11:5), but this is not the basis of sharing bread.

The next phrase carries all of the weight of the story. The neighbor will arise "because of his *anaideia*." Two mysteries must be solved. First, who does "his" refer to—the neighbor or the host? Traditional interpretations point to the surprised host—but the Greek text is ambiguous. Second, what is the meaning of this word *anaideia*? This is undoubtedly what motivates someone in the story to act.

(1) Notice how the NIV interprets the passage for us: "I tell you, though he will not get up and give him the bread because he is his friend, yet because of the man's boldness he will get up and give him as much as he needs." The NIV inserts the words "the man's" to point to the host as the subject of "his." The TNIV barely improves this by inserting the word "your": "because of *your* shameless audacity." *But this is not in the original text either.* Furthermore, the NIV translates *anaideia* as "boldness"—the host is bold in his request—as the key to gaining needed bread. However, this may not be the best translation. (Fortunately the TNIV supplies a footnote that straightens things out.) Many scholars today believe that "his" does not refer to the host but to the neighbor in bed.

(2) Added to this is the now widely discussed meaning of the Greek word *anaideia* so critical to the story. Traditional translators have said it means "shameless" or "persistent" (hence "bold") and that it is the virtue belonging to the surprised host. But this sense of the word comes only much later than the first century. In Greek, *aideia* (or its adjective *aidos*) means "shame" and the prefix *an* negates it. Thus *an-aideia* means *shameless* or better, "without shame."

In the Middle Eastern cultural context shame is the very thing you sought to avoid with all of our life. Honor—the absence of shame—was the attribute for which you wished to be known. You gathered honor to your family and you distributed honor to your community. Therefore we might easily say that someone in the story is a person in whom there is no shame, someone of honor, someone who recognizes and protects his good name and reputation.

Now suddenly Jesus' story takes on new meaning: "Yet because of *his lack of shame* he will rise and give him whatever he needs." *The parable is focused entirely on the neighbor in bed!* The request for bread (no persistence is suggested) is now something that will succeed *because of the sleeping neighbor's being asked.* Let's attempt a paraphrase of Luke 11:8:

I tell you, the sleeping neighbor will not get up and give his friend the bread because they are friends. The neighbor will get up and give fresh bread because he is a man of honor—a man who will not bring shame to himself or his village.

Suddenly Jesus' story turns on a new theme. Fresh bread for a surprise visitor will come through the door not because of the nature of the request or the relationship with the neighbor. This confident request is anchored to the honor of the neighbor in bed. Because he is a person of good character, bread will appear.

In Jesus' view, prayer (as requests from God) may be made confidently not because of who we are—but because of who he is. The character of God rather than our performance is at the center of Jesus' understanding of prayer. Our assurance does not spring from the quality of our request but from who God is. Because God has honor, he will attend to our needs.

A Father's Gifts

Our confidence that this is the correct interpretation of the story is confirmed if we keep reading Luke 11:9–13. Jesus is still explaining his view about prayer:

So I say to you: Ask and it will be given to you; seek and you will find; knock and the door will be opened to you. For everyone who asks receives; those who seek find; and to those who knock, the door will be opened.

Which of you fathers, if your son asks for a fish, will give him a snake instead? Or if he asks for an egg, will give him a scorpion? If you then, though you are evil, know how to give good gifts to your children, how much more will your Father in heaven give the Holy Spirit to those who ask him!

Jesus encourages us to ask, seek, and knock because these requests will be met by a God who is good. To illustrate, he offers two scenarios. First, if a son asks for a fish, what father would give him a snake? Jesus may have in mind eel-like fish that live at the bottom of the Sea of Gali-

A scorpion from Israel

lee, which were unclean and prohibited to Jews. *No father would give such a gift!* Then Jesus describes a son asking for an egg. Some scorpions in the Middle East can fold themselves so they appear to have an egg-shaped shell. *No father would give such a gift!* Matthew's gospel (Matt. 7:7–11) gives an extended version of this and adds one more scenario. If a son were to ask for bread, would his father give him a stone? It may be that Jesus is thinking about how baked bread is similar in size and color to eroded limestone in the Judean wilderness. *No father would give such a gift!*

Here is where this leads: if fathers who are imperfect, fallen, and sinful understand what it means to be attentive and responsive to their children's needs, *how much more* responsive will God be in all his goodness?

Faith and Prayer

The touchstone of Jesus' teaching about prayer is simple. It does not matter when we come to God in prayer (the unexpected guest came at midnight). Our need is foremost on God's mind. He will hear and he will listen, not because we have made ourselves exceptionally worthy, nor because we have used the right words or energy, cajoling him to give us what we want. God will answer because of who he is—good, righteous, and honorable.

Gary M. Burge

Near the ancient fortress of Machaerus, Jordan

Jesus answers the disciples' request—"Lord, teach us to pray"—and then takes up a small series of elements. We should pray in our own language with sincerity. We should pray with seriousness ("Ask! Seek! Knock!"). And knowing the God to whom we pray is more important than knowing how to construct prayers of persuasion and eloquence.

Chapter 3

STORIES ABOUT EXCUSES

Luke 14:15–24

IT WAS common for Jesus to tell stories that inspired a crisis or even a confrontation. He wasn't afraid to raise the tension in a conversation if he felt that a person's motives were hollow or dishonest. He insisted with marked regularity that lives frequently needed examination, motives needed to be unmasked, and our reasons for being *religious people* needed to be understood.

In Luke 13–14 Jesus was heading to Jerusalem after a lengthy ministry in Galilee. As he approached the city, he began to have increasing contact with Jerusalem's religious leadership. These were men who had heard about his reputation as a popular village teacher. As scholars, they knew he failed to have the formal learning they possessed—and his reputation for questioning the authorities by now had been well established. They were curious about him and apprehensive.

THE BANQUET

One Sabbath he was invited to the home of a synagogue ruler. Luke notes that their intentions were less than charitable ("he was being carefully watched," Luke 14:1), and in the middle of the

A RECONSTRUCTED FIRST CENTURY MEAL IN NAZARETH

Todd Bolen/www.BiblePlaces.com. Used by permission of Nazareth Village. www.nazarethvillage.com

event a severely ill man appeared before him. Jesus' reputation for breaking the Sabbath *as an act of religious duty* must have preceded him. Therefore Jesus took advantage of the situation.

Everyone at the table knew that work on the Sabbath was forbidden, and Jewish law made an exception only when life and death crises occurred. Therefore Jesus asked his hosts, "Is it lawful to heal on the Sabbath or not?" Such "work" should be technically forbidden because it did not "save life." But they sensed a trap and refused to answer.

Jesus promptly healed the man, sent him away, and offered the following question: If you have a son or even an ox that falls into a well on the Sabbath, would you not *immediately* pull him out? *Of course they would.* Yet the precedent that this set would undermine the laws the Pharisees defended that forbad Sabbath work. But for Jesus works of charity and compassion were the very works the Sabbath should promote. On another parallel occasion, Jesus was angry with such religious leaders because of their inability to see the truth in this (Mark 3:5).

It is at this moment that Jesus slipped into the role for which he was so famous. He became the evening's storyteller. Because he was at a banquet, the banquet setting seemed ideal for three new stories: the first spoke about humility and posturing when entering social engagements (Luke 14:7–11) and a second inquired about motives for making social overtures to people of influence (14:12–14). Virtues of humility and generosity should hallmark life, not the pursuit of social prestige. Generosity to the poor will be rewarded by God at the resurrection while generosity to the well-placed and self-important will only benefit us now.

Jesus' reference to God immediately inspired one guest to redirect the table conversation to religious subjects. "Blessed are those who will eat at the feast in the kingdom of God" (Luke 14:15). This is a formal, ancient Jewish phrase that today we might well translate, "Blessed are those who are saved!" The question now on the table held a sharper edge: Who will be a part of God's heavenly banquet? Will the guest list surprise us?

The Great Banquet

The story that Jesus tells in Luke 14:15–24 has suffered great misunderstanding. Jesus describes a banquet in which

A BIBLICAL MEAL AT "NAZARETH VILLAGE," GALILEE

many are being invited to come and join. *Yet in the history of interpretation we have seen ourselves as the banquet hosts and the world as potential guests.* Therefore the story has become a story about evangelism. But it is not. It is a sobering story with a sharp warning.

> *Jesus replied: "A certain man was preparing a great banquet and invited many guests. At the time of the banquet he sent his servant to tell those who had been invited, 'Come, for everything is now ready.' "*

The banquet was one of the oldest Jewish images for Israel's final communion with God. The banquet's lavish food and wine represented the overwhelming joy and abundance that would greet God's people in heaven or even here on the earth (Psalm 23:5; Isaiah 25:6–8). When many Jews—such as those at the Dead Sea community of Qumran—thought about the coming of the Messiah, they likewise thought about a banquet. It would be a party—a wedding banquet, perhaps—unlike anything seen before.

A variety of assumptions from the ancient Middle East shape this story.

Z. Radovan/www.BibleLandPictures.com

STORAGE JARS AND COOKING IMPLEMENTS, SEPPHORIS, GALILEE

Z. Radovan/www.BibleLandPictures.com

A LOW BANQUET TABLE WITH SHARED BOWLS

In Jesus' account, the man is hosting not simply an average banquet, but something great. No doubt his listeners imagined a luxurious room with low tables surrounded by cushions. It would be a banquet that everyone in the village would know about. A banquet talked about for months. A banquet whose invitation was priceless.

But we learn in the story that the banquet host invites many people who find they cannot attend. In our Western tradition, we believe that such excuses as these must be acceptable. However, such an assumption leads to a complete misunderstanding of the story.

In the village culture of Jesus' day, two invitations commonly went out to the community. In a culture where honor and shame were carefully weighed, a banquet host would not wish to sponsor a party when another family was planning one. *This would bring shame.* Nor would he want to host a party only to discover that many could not attend. *This too would bring shame.* In the story, the servant has gone out to call those "who had been invited." This means that the public calendar has been cleared, there are no competing village events—and that the invited guests have already been asked to come. *And above all, they have agreed to come.* Now all that remains is for the servant to approach them to tell them that all preparations are ready.

Three Excuses

The story, however, takes an unexpected turn. Rather than hearing that the privileged guests of the banquet have attired themselves in festive garments and immediately follow the servant, we learn that a series of excuses come from them. In each case, the reason for the denial is given, an interfering obligation or desire is explained, and a plea is offered. To understand these excuses, we must hear them as Jesus' earliest Middle Eastern audience heard them.

> *But they all alike began to make excuses. The first said, "I have just bought a field, and I must go and see it. Please excuse me."*
>
> *Another said, "I have just bought five yoke of oxen, and I'm on my way to try them out. Please excuse me."*
>
> *Still another said, "I just got married, so I can't come."*

(1) The real estate excuse. The villages of the Middle East—both in antiquity and today—take enormous care in the exchange of land. In ancient Jewish culture land was a legacy that belonged to a family (and a tribe) and therefore could not be sold casually. Even today this is true. Land is a person's identity. Land is named, trees are old, and they have stories attached to them; even hills and terraces are intimately familiar.

Notice, for example, how in Genesis Abraham does not simply settle in the city of Hebron—he lives at the "oaks of Mamre" (Gen. 13:18), and later he buries his wife Sarah in the "cave in the field of Machpelah" (23:19) near "Ephron's field" (23:17). Ancient Arab communities that have been in the Middle East for over a thousand years would know these instincts

David Bivin/www.LifeintheHolyLand.com

The Tomb of the Patriarchs built by Herod I, Hebron

well. No villager buys land that is distant and cannot be known or seen. Village land and the history of its owners are an integral part of village life. (This explains why conflicts over the taking of land are so explosive in modern Israel and Palestine.) As Westerners we barely understand this profound attachment to land.

Library of Congress, LC-matpc-05921/www.LifeintheHolyLand.com

Yoked oxen from the 19th century

Therefore this banquet guest has not produced a plausible excuse. He is not a Westerner who makes a quick purchase of land through an agent for investment. He is a man who buys land only after he has walked over it hill after hill until he knows every piece of it perfectly. Then he bargains for it for days. It is impossible that he would buy land and "not have seen it." *This is insulting.* The only possible excuse might sound like this: "I have been in negotiation for two months with my neighbor Moshe for the fields south of the eastern terraces, near Samuel's oak tree. And he insists we settle tonight. I beg you to excuse me."

A man who originally agreed to attend the banquet is now saying "No." And his excuse is an abrupt and shocking insult. *No honorable guest would ever act like this.* The banquet host has been dishonored.

(2) The plowing excuse. The second guest now produces a second lie. He says that he has just invested a considerable sum in oxen used for plowing, and he must now go and try them out. Therefore he cannot come.

Again the Middle East both today and in antiquity followed traditions associated with the purchase of work animals. The value of a team of oxen is linked directly to their ability to pull the plow together, to work cooperatively under the yoke, and to be controllable. In village life one never purchases such a team *without trying them out*. A farmer who is selling a team may announce the day he intends to use them, so that all would-be purchasers can come and watch. Or he may bring them to the edge of the village and invite any who wish to drive them. The key is here: testing comes before buying. In our culture it would be the same as if I declined an invitation at the last minute saying, "I have just bought a used car over the phone and I need to go see if it will start." *Testing precedes buying.*

Therefore in this second excuse, the banquet host is dishonored again. There can be no circumstance in which an animal comes before the obligation to attend a prepared banquet. This man who had once agreed to attend the banquet, who once said "Yes," is now saying "No." *No honorable guest would ever act like this.* And again the host is shocked and shamed.

(3) The marriage excuse. In each of the excuses seen thus far, the man says what he has done (e.g., "bought a field") and then what he is obligated to do ("go and see it"). This is followed by a respectful entreaty, "Please excuse me." This third episode elevates the offense to an unexpected level.

Middle Eastern cultures have always shown remarkable restraint when talking about women. Gender boundaries are strictly enforced and women are carefully guarded from contact with men who are unrelated to them. A woman's veil was in part the culture's attempt to enforce such modesty and discretion.

Todd Bolen/www.Bible-aces.com

AN ORTHODOX JEWISH WEDDING IN ISRAEL

A brilliant example of this tendency is found in the Jacob stories of Genesis. When Jacob arranges to marry his uncle's daughter Rachel, he attends his own wedding banquet, consummates the marriage, and only in the morning learns that the woman who is his wife is actually Leah, Rachel's older sister (Genesis 29:16–30).

Clearly Jacob barely knew his bride throughout the banquet! And never "saw" her till morning. How can this happen? Clearly Leah was thoroughly veiled so that her modesty would be protected.

This third excuse comes from a man who does not understand restraint in personal sexual matters. In a culture that barely refers to women in literature (notice how rarely women are named in the Old Testament), this man uses his wedding as an excuse. We may assume that this man has recently married, though we cannot think that this man's wedding was on the same day as the great banquet. *Avoiding such a conflict was the basis of the first invitation!*

This man even uses a lewd suggestion: "I cannot attend the wedding because I have just married [his reason]—and now I want to [his desire]. . . ." With delicate mastery of style, Jesus let's the man's voice go silent, but the sexual connotation is inevitable. This is a man so obsessed with his new bride that he would rather pursue the intimate privileges of that relationship than attend the banquet.

Note as well that while the other guests have used polite forms of appeal ("Please excuse me"), this man shows no such honor: "I can't come." This is a culture where honor-giving titles are used in abundance. This is a culture where denials are *always* prefaced with self-deprecating words. This is a world where a person rarely speaks boldly or rudely but rather uses indirect pleas to seek permissions. "I cannot come" is abrupt, shocking, unacceptable. *No honorable guest would ever act like this.* Once again the host has been shamed.

The Great Solution

In Jesus' story, a crisis has been built. An honorable member of the village has done everything right. He has prepared a feast; he has chosen the day. We have no evidence to think he has done anything other than what the village expects. The village knows the day of the banquet and the guests have given their RSVP to the servants. They plan to come. Yet, at this turning point of the story, the focus falls on three persons who give illegitimate excuses for their absence. The excuses are not merely *white lies* that may be overlooked. *They are insulting within the context of Jesus' world.*

But the banquet host has a solution. Just as there were gender boundaries in this culture, there were social boundaries marking who belong to a group—and who do not. Village life in ancient Israel was organized along tribal and regional lines. To be from Galilee was different than being from Judea. To marry someone from a village fifty miles away was unusual. Affiliations with Jewish outsiders were handled with care and connections with Gentile foreigners were handled with caution.

> *The servant came back and reported this to his master. Then the owner of the house became angry and ordered his servant, "Go out quickly into the streets and alleys of the town and bring in the poor, the crippled, the blind and the lame."*
>
> *"Sir," the servant said, "what you ordered has been done, but there is still room."*
>
> *Then the master told his servant, "Go out to the roads and country lanes and compel them to come in, so that my house will be full. I tell you, not one of those who were invited will get a taste of my banquet."*

In the story the banquet host tells his servant to solicit the interest of two new groups in order to compensate for the dishonoring behavior of his guests. First, he should invite those in the streets and lanes of the city—the poor and the handicapped.

THE LEPERS AND THE POOR IN 19TH CENTURY JERUSALEM

This first venue describes those who are a part of village life but who live on the margin; they are deemed socially "low" and would never get an opportunity for such an invitation. They are no doubt surprised by the request to come and wonder why those with the usual social connections are refusing.

The servant reports that these have already come in, but there is still room at the banquet. At this point, the host makes a remarkable decision. He directs the servant to go further out—beyond the village boundaries—and invite in those who are outsiders. These are likely people from other families unknown to the village. Or more shocking still, these may be Gentiles who lived alongside but rarely among the Jews of Jesus' day. This host wants his banquet to be full, and he is angry that those who once said yes to his invitation are now refusing to come.

The tension of the story is reinforced in the story's final sentence. Jesus breaks character with the storyteller's role and seems to address his listeners directly. "I tell you" is here in the plural. No longer is this the voice of the host addressing his hard-working servant. *This is the voice of Jesus speaking to the gathered Pharisees.* Those invited—you who have been invited—will never taste *my banquet* if the circumstances of this story continue to prevail.

Faith and the Great Banquet

In this remarkably brief narrative, Jesus has placed a challenge on the banquet table of his first-century host and his guests. *This is not the only banquet handing out invitations this day.* God has announced that his messianic banquet is beginning—the kingdom of God is at hand! In Jesus' setting, those Jews who are listening, who have lived lives of faithfulness and commitment, who have demonstrated their "yes" to God by their beliefs and lifestyle, must now decide if they will join God's banquet. *An empty excuse is no excuse.*

This is a timeless message whose edge brings discomfort to Christians just as easily as anyone else. The hour has come. Jesus is announcing the banquet. Only one question remains: Will we step into the banquet, or will we manufacture dishonoring reasons why we cannot come? Christian life and identity can be as fossilized and unyielding as anything in Judaism. To discover what God is doing today in Christ inspires the same temptation as those in the first century. Will we act faithfully and join Christ or produce excuses that betray our lack of faith?

Chapter 4

STORIES ABOUT COMPASSION

Luke 10:25–37

JESUS OFTEN told stories that probed core values at the heart of people's lives. Was religion a passport to social prestige? Was it a habit, a tradition inherited at an early age and rarely weighed? Was it grounded in an experience of the goodness of God or was it directed by fear and law? And what role did compassion and humility play in spiritual identities?

Christian writer Dallas Willard has made the astute observation that one reason the church may lack vitality and conviction today is that it is too often in the business of sin management. We live with a "bar-code" mentality thinking that our religious lives will in some manner guarantee our entry to heaven—that our set of beliefs or our religious experiences will pass some test and guarantee us eternal life. And that's the point of church attendance.

Jesus was less interested in the guarantee of heaven and more keenly interested in discipleship. How we live in relation to God in this world came before how we might live in eternity. Of course eternal life was an important theme for him, but once obtained, the immediate follow-up question had to do with the way spiritual life formed how we live. For

THE GREAT JUDEAN WILDERNESS LOOKING EAST
Todd Bolen/www.BiblePlaces.com

example, he rarely talked about creeds or belief systems that defined the center of the kingdom of God. He only said that we must make him Lord—and then goes on quickly to talk about demonstrating how much we love him by how we obey him. Matthew 7:21 is typical: "Not everyone who says to me, 'Lord, Lord,' will enter the kingdom of heaven, but only those who do the will of my Father who is in heaven." Again, Matthew 7:24: "Therefore everyone who hears these words of mine and puts them into practice is like a wise man who built his house on the rock."

An Opening Enquiry

An interesting episode that illustrates these themes begins in Luke 10:25, where Jesus is approached by an "expert in the law" or "lawyer" who wants to test his theological ability. We should not think of this as a criminal or civil attorney as we think about them today. In Jesus' world, criminal, civil, and religious law ran together. Religious leaders were equally legal consultants. This title for this man (Greek, *nomikos*) implies that he may be a Pharisee—or more likely he is a priest who serves as a legal expert when not working at the temple. This latter connection is interesting since in the story that follows, temple workers play a significant role.

The unnamed lawyer approaches Jesus respectfully and uses a dignified title for him ("teacher"). He even stands before Jesus, yet another sign of respect. All of this is surprising, for he is a professional teacher of the law—and here he is addressing a respected layperson. It was as unusual then as it would be today.

His enquiry is simple: What *must be done* to gain eternal life? In about AD 90, another teacher named Rabbi Eliezer was asked the same question, "Rabbi, teach us the ways of life so that by them we may attain the life of the future world" (Bab. Talmud, *Berakot* 28b). He presumed that there was a way of living that would so please God that it necessarily led to a life in eternity with God. In Jesus' case, this conversation leads to "two rounds" with the lawyer, which need to be followed carefully.

Jesus' first response is precisely what we might expect of a rabbi. "What is written in the Law?" The law (or as we might

Z. Radovan/www.BibleLandPictures.com

A Jewish mezuzah in Jerusalem holding a household scroll

understand it, "the Scripture") is God's direction for life. Jesus challenges the lawyer to distill the message of the Scriptures, and he does so expertly. He cites Deuteronomy 6:4–5, the second half of Israel's great creed, "Hear, O Israel: The LORD our God, the LORD is one. Love the LORD your God with all your heart and with all your soul and with all your strength."

These words were fundamental to Israel's life. They were spoken morning and evening. Along with the Ten Commandments (Deut. 5) they were often written on small scrolls and placed on doorposts, worn on the forehead and on the arm in ceremonial leather straps (Hebrew, *tefillin*), and integrated into liturgies of home and synagogue. To these sacred words the lawyer makes his own addition from Leviticus 19:18, "*Love your neighbor as yourself.*" It is a thoughtful and reflective touch.

Jesus clearly likes his response and commends him (Luke 10:28). But there is a deeper question that now surfaces, and

Library of Congress, LC-matpc-03893/www.LifeintheHolyLand.com

Jewish phylacteries or tefillin in Israel

Jesus is prepared for it. It is one thing to recite creeds or verses from the Bible. It is quite another thing to live a life that embraces the themes of those creeds.

The lawyer now possesses Jesus' endorsement of his answer and then opens a second round of discussion. He is a minimalist and is curious about the limits of his religious obligations (Luke says that "he wanted to justify himself"). He sees that loving God and loving others are necessary—but how far does it go? Who should be classified as *his neighbor*?

Todd Bolen/www.BiblePlaces.com

A Jewish mezuzah with its scripture scroll

Thanks to the oppression of Greek, then Roman occupations, Judaism debated the meaning of the "neighbor" it was obligated to love in Leviticus 19:18. Non-Israelites were excluded; Pharisees excluded non-Pharisees; one later rabbinic saying taught that heretics, informers, and renegades should be pushed into ditches and not retrieved. Still another popular teaching excluded personal enemies—an idea that Jesus rejected explicitly ("You have heard that it was said, 'Love your neighbor and hate your enemy.' But I tell you, love your enemies and pray for those who persecute you," Matt. 5:43–44). The lawyer wants to know how wide is the sweep of Jesus' interest. *Whom are we obligated to love?*

The Wounded Man and the Samaritan

In this second round, Jesus responds with a story. The important answer for the lawyer is not the content of his belief but the manner of his life. And Jesus expertly crafts a story to present the problem in an unexpected way. The question for Jesus is no longer "who qualifies as neighbor." *It is something else.*

> *A man was going down from Jerusalem to Jericho, when he fell into the hands of robbers. They stripped him of his clothes, beat him and went away, leaving him half dead.*

The seventeen-mile road from Jerusalem to Jericho is remote, difficult, and dangerous—well known as notorious by many ancient writers. It descends 3,600 feet in a short span and even today remnants of the old Roman road (along the Wadi Qilt gorge, above Jericho) assumed in the story can still be found. Jesus describes a man traveling here alone—something that was certainly foolish. Like wandering New York City alone at midnight, anyone who is robbed might be asked, *What did you expect?*

This man is robbed, stripped, beaten, and left unconscious ("half dead") on the roadside. At once the story takes on an intriguing idea: *the man is naked*. His social status and nationality cannot be identified by clothes or speech. He is a raw human in need—and that is all we know.

> *A priest happened to be going down the same road, and when he saw the man, he passed by on the other side. So too, a Levite, when he came to the place and saw him, passed by on the other side.*

Threefold stories were common in Judaism and Jesus now spins one with a surprise. The first two characters were servants of the temple in Jerusalem. Since they are going *down* the road, we are to understand that they have just completed their service at the temple. First, we meet a priest. Jerusalem had

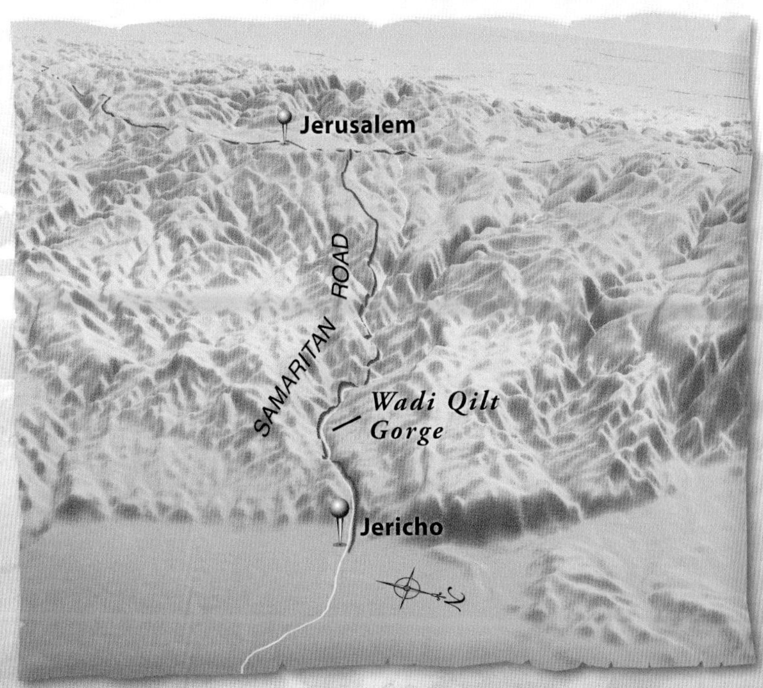

Todd Bolen/www.BiblePlaces.com

THE PATH OF THE ANCIENT ROMAN ROAD FROM JERUSALEM TO JERICHO

twenty-four rotations of priests, each serving the temple for two weeks. He has just finished his rotation and is now headed home. Because of his upper-class status, the story presupposes that he is riding a donkey and likely has a small entourage of friends and guards with him. We cannot assume he is walking (only the poor walk seventeen miles in the desert) and is thus unable to render aid. We only hear an explicit reference to a donkey later with the Samaritan. Thus the priest has all the equipment found later in the story. He *could have done* what the Samaritan will do.

When the priest sees the unconscious man, he passes by on the other side of the road. Some scholars believe that he thinks the man is dead and fears "corpse impurity" (based on Lev. 21:1). A priest could not touch a corpse (except for his immediate family) or else he would incur a status of "unclean," making it impossible to serve at the temple. But since the priest is headed *away* from Jerusalem, he may be less worried about impurity. However, his ability to enjoy his status and obtain the income of tithes would have ended. Either way, this man represents the highest order of religious life in Israel. He (or a servant) could have at least probed the man to see if he were alive. *But he does not act in compassion.*

Remarkably Jesus' audience would not have judged the priest. The priest is shaped by a world that judges clean and unclean regularly, creating hierarchies and catalogues of those who are pure and those who are impure, those acceptable and unacceptable, those "inside" and "outside." He is thus *above* these troubles. A Jewish saying urges, "If you do a kindness, know to whom you do it. . . . Give to the godly man, but do not help the sinner" (Sir. 12:1–4).

Next we learn that a Levite is traveling the same road. Levites were clerical aids at the temple and they too had rules associated with touching corpses. However, their rules were less stringent (they observed ritual cleanliness only during temple service). Thousands of these men worked at the temple and people saw them as knowledgeable and respected clerical leaders. However, this Levite does the same as the priest: *he comes, he sees, and he passes by*. Again a man with considerable religious importance, a man who certainly knows the law and practices it scrupulously does not act in compassion.

In the third step of the story, Jesus' listeners expect him to introduce a Jewish layperson—a man without religious credentials, but nevertheless an honorable Jewish layperson. This is a descending catalogue of characters: priest, Levite, citizen. A dramatic ending might have even placed a peasant

A caravan of camels from 19th century Ottoman Palestine

in the story as hero. But instead, Jesus introduces a *Samaritan* as a man who comes by, sees, *and acts with compassion*.

Library of Congress, LC-matpc-01862/www.LifeintheHolyLand.com

A Samaritan family eating their Passover meal

> *But a Samaritan, as he traveled, came where the man was; and when he saw him, he took pity on him. He went to him and bandaged his wounds, pouring on oil and wine. Then he put the man on his own donkey, took him to an inn and took care of him. The next day he took out two denarii and gave them to the innkeeper. "Look after him," he said, "and when I return, I will reimburse you for any extra expense you may have."*

To understand the shock of this turn of events, we must understand that the Samaritans were a despised ethnic group

Todd Bolen/www.BiblePlaces.com

The Byzantine ruins on Mt. Gerizim, once the site of the Samaritan Temple

living north of Jerusalem. The tensions between them and Jerusalem began in the Old Testament when the northern and southern kingdoms split. But it continued for almost a thousand years and led to overt hostility in Jesus' day. Once Jewish soldiers had destroyed the Samaritan temple. Then one night in AD 6, the Samaritans returned the favor by defiling the temple at Passover, scattering human bones throughout the sanctuary and stopping all worship.

The Samaritan is likely a merchant leaving Jerusalem following business (why else is he so far from Samaria?). He has money, a donkey, wine, and oil—all items a man of means might possess. Later we learn that the innkeeper in Jericho knows him so well that he trusts him to return and finish his bill. This is a business traveler who frequents this road.

The "Good Samaritan Inn" as it served travelers in the 19th century

And he can make no religious claims. In fact, the Samaritan priests rejected the Jerusalem temple (John 4:20) and disputed the Jewish law. In many respects, he is disqualified immediately as a candidate for religious heroism. In fact, he is precisely the sort of man who would not recite the creed so carefully uttered earlier by the lawyer.

Nevertheless he does exactly what those from Jerusalem have not done. He identifies whether the man is alive, and if we assume he does not carry bandages, he likely uses his clothing (his head cloth or linen undergarment) to wrap the man's wounds, and he uses oil and wine as medicinal treatments. From this point, the Samaritan walks all the way to Jericho while the wounded man rides and there finds an inn;

he pulls out money to use for his recovery. A day's stay at an inn would cost one-twelfth of a denarius. The Samaritan supplies two denarii—twenty-four days' worth of care—and even guarantees more money if it is needed.

Z. Radovan/www.BibleLandPictures.com

Two Roman denarii from the New Testament era

The Unexpected Question

Now Jesus turns the question of "neighbor" on its head. The lawyer has asked the wrong question. The lawyer originally wanted to assess those who owned the status of "neighbor" around him, who then held him to some moral obligation. He was organizing his world and making some assessment of religious obligations. There were those who qualified as his neighbor—and those who did not. But Jesus ignores the worldview entirely.

> *"Which of these three do you think was a neighbor to the man who fell into the hands of robbers?"*
>
> *The expert in the law replied, "The one who had mercy on him."*
>
> *Jesus told him, "Go and do likewise."*

"Neighbor" is not a title owned by those who live beyond us—*neighbor is a title that may or may not describe us*. The question is not who is the lawyer's neighbor; the question is whether the lawyer himself is a neighbor, whether he behaves with love rather than builds a world that sorts out those whom he will or will not love.

Faith and the Samaritan

Religion builds a worldview. And with our religious convictions we are able to locate ourselves in relation to God, the world, other believers, and "outsiders"—those who have no interest in our beliefs. It is easy enough to find common interests with those who share our faith. "Insiders" recognize and respect other "insiders."

However, religion can also become a means to justify harsh treatment of "outsiders." They have failed morally. Or they have failed to show spiritual commitment. Or they may believe things that our own circle of faith repudiates. Whatever the inspiration, many religious worldviews create a hierarchy of those who ought to be genuinely loved—and those for whom love is at best optional.

In December 2000 I was given the remarkable invitation by Shaykh Ahmad Kuftaro, the late Grand Mufti of Syria, to speak during Friday prayers at the influential Abu Nour Mosque in Damascus. Kuftaro and his Damascus mosque are famous throughout the country. Many questions rushed through my mind. *What should I say? What lines were being crossed? Do evangelicals normally speak in Muslim mosques, particularly when it is covered by Syrian TV?*

I chose to speak on Jesus' parable of the good Samaritan. This choice came initially because the parable spoke to me about my own willingness to "cross the road" and be with Muslims. But more, it was a universal message that could speak to Muslims as well—Muslims whose faith gave them an immediate respect for Jesus and the gospel. And here in Syria there lived about one million Christians (5 percent of the population), whose relationship with Muslims was often strained. The true test of faith—any faith—I argued, was how it treats those whom it deems to be "outsiders." This is a challenge for Christians as well as Muslims. I remember speaking in the great mosque, Sheikh Kuftaro nodding in agreement, and the huge kneeling audience in rapt attention. After telling the parable I concluded:

> *Being "neighbor" is meaningless if it only refers to those inside my cultural or national or religious circle. Being "neighbor" means that I look inside my American world and embrace those who are different than me: African Americans, Hispanics, Asians, Arabs. Being neighbor is about courage, about taking risks; it is about walking across the road and helping—and not using religion as an excuse to stay away.*
>
> *If Jesus were to tell this story in Syria today, who would be its characters? Who would have the courage to cross over the road, to embrace those who are different? This is one reason I am interested in the amazing history of Syria. Here you have many different communities with*

rich and ancient histories. And as those communities live together, crossing the road, they fulfill one of the great commandments of Jesus.

Later that afternoon I joined a group of Christians at the Greek Catholic Patriarchy of Damascus and there listened to His Grace Bishop Assador Batecha. I was inspired by his brilliance and his faith. But he told us boldly the same message I had just given to the Muslims at Abu Nour. I took notes to remember. Speaking for the Arab world, he told us plainly how the Middle East hears the language of Christian faith and wholesome values and democracy coming from America, but cannot "see" gestures of good will, righteousness, and charity. Our immoral media and our weapons sales betray us, he argued. He finished: "Muslims will not read your American books or listen to your speeches; but they will *see you*. And the one question is this: What does the world see when it sees you?"

In 2007 I was invited to return to Damascus to speak to a large gathering of Syrian Christians. Just to the east a war in Iraq was worsening daily. Already a million Iraqi refugees had fled to Syria. Could it destabilize Syria? Would it jeopardize the safe life of the Christians there? Should the Christians see these fleeing Muslims as a threat? Or was this an opportunity? I read again the parable of the good Samaritan, remembering once more the words of Bishop Batecha spoken five years earlier to an American delegation: "Muslims will not read your books or listen to your speeches; *but they will see you. And the one question is this: What will they see?*"

Chapter 5

Stories of Forgiveness

Matthew 18:21–35

REVENGE CAN be a satisfying pursuit. Or at least this is what we tell ourselves. Someone offends us and our gut instinct is to answer the offense with a corresponding and sometimes stronger response. The reason we do this is not simply to return anger for anger—but to correct the imagined harm someone has done to our property, our self-worth, or our standing in the community. Our opponent has assaulted something (our bodies? our reputation?), and the damage must be repaid by a corresponding act.

In Jesus' society revenge was not only common but it was viewed as legitimate. He lived in a world where a person's *honor* was preserved at all costs, and protecting that honor was an appropriate and necessary exercise. *This was the essence of revenge.* The Old Testament is filled with stories of revenge pursued violently. Following the attack on their sister Dinah, Simeon and Levi protected their family honor by attacking and killing the men of the city of Shechem (Gen. 34:25). Samson avenged the loss of his eyes at the hands of his Philistine captors by ripping down their pagan temple and killing countless soldiers (Judg. 16:28). Amnon was King David's oldest son and

Beth Shemesh monastery of Samson

Todd Bolen/www.BiblePlaces.com

David Bivin/www.LifeintheHolyLand.com

New excavations in Hebron, one of ancient Israel's cities of refuge

the crown prince—but when he raped his half-sister Tamar, Absalom reclaimed honor by killing him (2 Sam. 13:23–29).

These stories illustrate how the biblical world understood revenge. And it explains why it was necessary to build "cities of refuge" so that accusations could be weighed fairly and cycles of revenge would not go on continuously and rip apart Israelite society. Imagine a world with people and tribes waiting for their opportunity to avenge something done in the past.

Exhortations to refrain from honor-seeking revenge are also in the Bible. "Do not seek revenge or bear a grudge against anyone among your people, but love your neighbor as yourself. I am the Lord" (Lev. 19:18). "Do not say, 'I'll do to them as they have done to me; I'll pay them back for what they did' " (Prov. 24:29). Yet despite these exhortations, this society realized that revenge would follow a crime when revenge was pursued justly. "An eye for an eye" was a teaching echoed not only throughout the Bible (cf. Ex. 21:24, Lev. 24:20, Deut. 19:21) but one that is used today to justify vengeful reactions to those who have harmed us.

Jesus and Revenge

The greatest event of dishonoring violence in the New Testament is the cross of Christ. His suffering and public shaming is recorded as something so shocking that we expect even God to avenge it. And yet—this is central to the New Testament—the striking mercy of God is found in Jesus' forgiveness for his tormentors. "Father, forgive them" replaces "Father, punish them" as the call from Golgotha. If Christ was able to forgive even these violent people, so should we.

Forgiveness replacing revenge is a theme, however, that not only surfaces at the conclusion of Christ's life, but was central to his ministry. In the Sermon on the Mount, Jesus said, "You have heard that it was said, 'Eye for eye and tooth for tooth.' But I tell you, do not resist an evil person. If anyone slaps you on the right cheek, turn to them the other cheek also" (Matt. 5:38–39). Everyone in his audience knew what Jesus meant. The impulse to revenge is unacceptable. Mercy and forgiveness are to be the order of his disciples' life. Those who pursue and persecute must become a source of blessing rather than an agent for revenge (Matt. 5:11–12).

Scala/Art Resource, NY

THE CRUCIFIXION BY V. FOPPA (1425-1515)

This theme was so central to Jesus' world that he must speak to it regularly. In Matthew 18:15 Jesus comments on what to do if someone sins against you. The sense here implies a time when one person has dishonored or offended another, not simply when they have made some error. Jesus' instructions follow closely Jewish teaching: a private confrontation is followed by two witnesses—which (if all fails) is then brokered by the larger community. The result is not a counterbalancing of harm (revenge), but removal from the circle of Jesus' followers. If the offender accepts their guilt, there can be restoration. If this fails, there is separation.

The Forgiven Servant

The possibility that forgiveness could be without limit presents a problem for Peter (Matt. 5:21). Are we obligated to forgive someone even seven times? The common rabbinic maxim was that forgiveness was required three times, and Peter is far exceeding this. Jesus, however, responds with more: we should forgive seventy-seven times (or the Greek can read 7 times 70, or 490 times). This is an echo of a most remarkable commitment to revenge, noted in several places in the Old Testament: Cain will claim a sevenfold revenge, but Lamech will claim seventy-seven (or 7 times 70, Gen. 4:24). The point here is not that forgiveness should be tied to a number but that it should be unlimited. The exhausting unlimited revenge of Lamech is now balanced by the unlimited forgiveness of Christ's followers.

The Apostle Peter by F. del Cossa (1435-1477)

In order to make the point clearer, Jesus tells a story that expresses not only the extent of forgiveness but its grounding. New Testament scholar Kenneth Bailey has shown the artful structure of the story, which makes a stark comparison between two very different situations.

> *Therefore, the kingdom of heaven is like a king who wanted to settle accounts with his servants. As he began the settlement, a man who owed him ten thousand bags of gold was brought to him. Since he was not able to pay, the master ordered that he and his wife and his children and all that he had be sold to pay the debt.*
>
> *The servant fell on his knees before him. "Be patient with me," he begged, "and I will pay everything." The servant's master took pity on him, canceled the debt and let him go.*

The story imagines a Gentile king who is settling up with some of his clients within his realm. In Galilee such a picture—and its remarkable punishments—was imaginable since the land was ruled by Herod Antipas, whose government was not only ruthless but hard-pressed to find money within a poor Galilee population. These "servants" in the story are likely financial ministers, regional governors, or most likely men who worked collecting taxes from the population (called "tax farmers").

Such men were enormously powerful and wealthy, and they competed for tax collection licenses by bidding for such positions. They would promise (in their bid) to deliver an annual sum to the king—and even leave a pledge amount with him as a guarantee. Then it was up to this person, along with his many subministers, spies, and workers, to locate all wealth, raise taxes, and collect a surplus for his own profits.

In other words, this story is not about the collection of a personal debt. It is about large tax revenues a tax farmer owes the king—who in turn will likely deliver it to the Roman empire to appease its demands for the province.

One such tax client owes ten thousand "talents." This is absurd and makes the story humorous, even fantastic. The Greek term for this number is "myriad" (Gk. *murioi*) and simply means "beyond number," since it is the largest number

Z. Radovan/www.BibleLandPictures.com

A HORDE OF BYZANTINE GOLD COINS FOUND AT CAPERNAUM, GALILEE

Greek can express. It implies that this client owes more than anyone could imagine. A talent (also the largest measure) was a weighted amount, usually sixty-five to ninety-five pounds. According to a first-century Jewish historian (Josephus), a talent could equal ten thousand denarii, and a denarius was a Roman coin equal to a one-day's wage for a laborer. This means that the debt here was 100 million denarii. To put this in perspective, Josephus tells that in 4 B.C. the tax debt of the *entire country* (Galilee, Judea, Samaria) was *600 talents*! To put all of this in English, the client owed *billions of dollars* in a world that never saw that sort of money. This is hyperbole indeed!

But the tax client cannot produce the revenue to pay his contracted debt. Therefore he and his family are sold into slavery. This will in some measure satisfy the king's anger, but it will not recover the money. The most expensive slaves were sold for about one talent although most were sold for far less. According to Jewish law women and children could not be sold, but in the story this is a Gentile king, and he has none of the moral scruples held by Jewish rulers. No doubt the man's property is liquidated and sold as well. But despite these drastic measures, this debt is impossible. A laborer would have to work 250,000 years to earn a sufficient amount! In other words, the tax client's situation is utterly hopeless.

Therefore the client throws himself on the floor like a slave prostrating himself before the king, begging him for mercy. He pleads for patience and promises to pay "everything" to the king—a promise that is hardly credible given the amount.

Remarkably, the king cancels the debt.

Jesus says that the king was "felt compassion" (NASB)—the very same response we often find in Jesus himself. In Matthew 9:36 Jesus see the crowds and is moved with compassion. This is the emotional response that inspires him to feed the five thousand (14:14) and the four thousand (15:32). This is also the reaction of the good Samaritan when he sees the man on the roadside (Luke 10:33). Therefore out of compassion, the king acts in an utterly unexpected way: the debt is forgiven and the servant is released from prison.

The Unforgiving Servant

Kingdoms in the ancient world understood circumstances that halted tax payment. Wars or failed crops made payments impossible—and so tax revenues failed to come in. Torture or imprisonment—enforcement strategies well known in this era—simply could not produce income for a king no matter how severe the measures. When taxes were forgiven by Rome, there was a universal understanding that if Caesar was not being paid, so too lower levels of government—taxing clients in the empire—should likewise extend tax relief to their debtors.

This is made plain in tax collection laws we know from Hellenistic Egypt. Forgiveness should work its way down so that the provinces have an opportunity to recover. Thus a tax client who has enjoyed such benevolence *is obligated* to pass it on for the good of the kingdom. Surely the subject of our story, the surprised tax client, knows this principle.

> *But when that servant went out, he found one of his fellow servants who owed him a hundred silver coins. He grabbed him and began to choke him. "Pay back what you owe me," he demanded.*
>
> *His fellow servant fell to his knees and begged him, "Be patient with me, and I will pay you back."*

Hedda Gjerpen/www.istockphoto.com

The Roman Emperor Caesar Augustus

But he refused. Instead he went off and had the man thrown into prison until he could pay the debt.

Z. Radovan/www.BibleLandPictures.com

A Roman denarius

The story now takes an unexpected turn. The forgiven servant now exits the palace, sees a colleague, and confronts him. But who is this second servant? Two options are possible. He may be a subcontractor working for the first servant, who assesses taxes within his tax region and pays debts to him. In this case, the forgiveness of the king should have led the senior tax client to extend parallel forgiveness to his subcontractors. Another interpretation is more grim. This may be a tax farmer, a colleague, like the first client, a man standing in line waiting likewise to settle up with the king for his taxing area. And if this were a time of economic duress, he possesses the same problem as the first tax farmer.

But in this case, he happens to owe a personal debt to the first servant. One hundred denarii is a pittance compared with the debt the king is discussing. It is "few dollars" by comparison. The first debt was almost one million times more than this one. Nevertheless, the man is attacked and payment is demanded along with the threat of imprisonment. What is striking is that such a deed would be offensive to the king not because it lacked grace, but because it placed in prison a man who owed the king money. *This was not only an act of ingratitude but was a profound disservice to the royal treasury.* As a tax minister serving the king, he continued to serve even after his dismissal, and this deed shows his disloyalty.

The plea of the second servant parallels that of the first: "Be patient with me. . . ." The language is identical and may have been a speech planned for the king, but now must be used for a lesser minister. Yet, the first servant has no compassion and cannot even hear the echo of his own plea. Instead, he has the man jailed. Note how carefully both episodes share the same symmetry: a debt, consequences, an appeal, and resolution. In good story-telling fashion, the comparison is inevitable.

The Angry King

The anger of the first servant's colleagues comes as no surprise. These people see the injustice inflicted on their friend, they see the lack of charity, and they wonder if the same thing could happen to them.

> *When his other servants saw what had happened, they were greatly distressed and went and told their master everything that had happened.*
>
> *Then his master called the servant in. "You wicked servant," he said. "I canceled all that debt of yours because you begged me to. Shouldn't you have had mercy on your fellow servant just as I had on you?" In anger his master handed him over to the jailers to be tortured, until he should pay back all that he owed.*

Todd Bolen/www.BiblePlaces.com

A prison under Rome used since the 4th century B.C.

Their report to the king certainly retold this astonishing lack of gratitude, but more, their fellow servants were able to frame the tale as an example of disloyalty to the kingdom. What is the point of jailing people who would otherwise be collecting money for the king? And why interfere with the king's tax collection when such a small debt (a hundred denarii) was at stake?

The king's accusation and appeal follow rules well known from the ancient world. Debt forgiveness should extend to the lowest levels (since no one can pay). Here is a man who experienced generosity and yet cannot even mirror this generosity to another. The king finds it reprehensible and, as a result, reverses his decision and demands full payment of the original debt. Since the man's original jeopardy returns, he is immediately handed to the jailer.

It is incorrect to think that the king is motivated simply by the hypocrisy he finds in the ungrateful servant. The servant was released on the assumption that he would continue to serve faithfully and later address the issue of debt. But now he has shown himself unfaithful—even willing to disregard his master's financial well-being. Therefore he is no doubt removed from his position—his status as tax client is dissolved—and on

Todd Bolen/www.BiblePlaces.com

THE PATERNOSTER CHURCH, MT. OF OLIVES, JERUSALEM, SHOWING THE LORD'S PRAYER IN MOSAIC IN 62 DIFFERENT LANGUAGES.

this basis he simply becomes a debtor. *Because he misused his position (as evidenced through his behavior) he lost it, and he can no longer find shelter in the title he once enjoyed.*

Faith and Forgiveness

The idea that undergirds this parable is found in the Lord's Prayer: "Forgive us our debts as we also have forgiven our debtors" (Matt. 6:12). In Jesus' mind disciples must live a life that corresponds to what they have received from God. Few of his stories end with a specific application, but in this case Jesus provides his own clarification: "So my heavenly Father will also do to every one of you, if you do not forgive your brother or sister from your heart." Those who abuse God's forgiveness, who have not been affected by its power, prove in their own lives that they do not understand what it means to be forgiven.

AP Photo/Mahmoud Tawil

The wounds of civil war, Beirut, Lebanon

I began speaking about how common revenge was in Jesus' world. The same is true of the Middle East today. These cultural values have remained constants for two thousand years. But within this honor-protecting culture, there are astonishing opportunities for forgiveness.

Lebanon has witnessed over thirty-five years of breathtaking violence. Civil war (1975–1990), invasion and occupation by

Israel (1982), occupation by Syria (1990), and a recent devastating war with Israel (2006) has all but destroyed what was once the "Paris of the Middle East." This is a country that understands war.

During the chaos of the fighting in the 1980s, many villages were attacked by rival militias. In one village in the south, a Druze militia attacked a Christian village and massacred countless people. One eighteen-year-old girl named Mary lost thirty-three family members in one day. When Mary saw the killing, she fled the village desperate to get away. Druze soldiers gave chase, she fell, and one of them was on her immediately. A young man aimed a gun at Mary's face and simply said, "Renounce the cross or die." Mary responded, "I am a Christian and I will die a Christian." The gun fired and the bullet passed through her jaw and out her neck, destroying her spine. She was instantly a quadriplegic. The soldier then took out his knife and carved a cross on her chest—and left her to die.

The next day, the Druze soldiers wanted to take over the village completely. They collected the bodies, created a large pile, and awaited orders. Then one man heard a voice, the voice of Mary, whimpering from the body pile. Mary was removed, taken to a hospital, and given medical treatment.

Today Mary lives in a Lebanese home for the paralyzed. She has a little movement in her right arm, but all else has been lost. She paints watercolors and often will give them to visiting strangers.

Bob Seiple (who told me this story) visited Mary while he was the president of World Vision. The story overwhelmed him. "How do you handle this?" he asked her. "How do you live?"

Mary answered Bob, "I have forgiven my enemies because Christ has forgiven me. And I am looking for the man who hurt me so I can tell him I forgive him."

Bob will tell you he has never been the same since that conversation. If forgiveness and mercy are possible for a woman like Mary, it is possible for each one of us. Through her forgiving, she has been set free—free of anger, free to live without dreams of revenge and reprisal.

Extending God's grace—a grace we have already received—to others is the foremost hallmark of Christian identity. And if we take Jesus at his word here, it is deeply important to him.

Chapter 6

FINDING THE LOST

Luke 15

FIRST-CENTURY JEWISH society carefully measured "insiders" and "outsiders." Its strong cultural habits, its religious dietary restrictions, its reflex to mark who were "clean" and "unclean," and its rigorous separation from Gentiles each contributed to an instinct that parsed the world with considerable zeal.

Of course, not everyone agreed. Some Jews decided to live outside Judea—Alexandria or Rome perhaps—and this was sometimes viewed as an unacceptable mixing with the non-Jewish world. Other Jews mixed fully with Gentiles, sometimes adopting their dress, food, and language. Our earliest pictorial image of Jews comes from a fourth-century synagogue in Dura-Europas, located along the Euphrates River in northeast Syria. Beautiful wall frescoes show third-century Jews—along with Abraham and Jacob!—wearing Roman clothing and haircuts. (The frescoes can be seen today in the Syrian National Museum in Damascus.)

This question of "separation" was a major issue of debate in Judea and Galilee in Jesus' day. The penetration of Hellenistic culture into Judaism gave rise to increasing concerns about identifying those who were "insiders" to pious Jewish culture.

SHEEP ON A HILLSIDE
Todd Bolen/www.BiblePlaces.com

Z. Radovan/www.BibleLandPictures.com

Wall murals from the Dura Europas Synagogue, Syria

The same can be seen today in the United States. Orthodox Jewish communities in New York and Chicago realize that their survival depends on maintaining their cultural integrity, keeping strong boundaries with Gentiles living around them as well as retaining those habits that serve as public markers for identity (dress, diet, schools, etc.).

More liberal (Reform) Jews find such rules restricting, while neighboring Gentiles find them bewildering and occasionally offensive. Imagine inviting orthodox Jews over for dinner only to have them announce what they cannot eat and then bring along their own dishes and cutlery, lest they eat with (unclean) Gentile utensils. Separation clearly brings its social challenges.

In a culture that values separation, one principal problem arises. How do we treat those on the far margin (Gentiles) and those on the near margin (lapsed Jews)? What happens to those whose choices, often poor choices, make them unacceptable to the values of "insiders"? Should they be scorned and rejected?

Luke 15 begins with a description of Jesus' social world—a world not entirely favorable among those who were in religious leadership. "Tax collectors" and "sinners" have begun following Jesus, but he does not reject them. The former were profiting from their collaboration with the Roman occupation of the country. The Romans used a method of tax collection called "tax farming," where they sold the ability to gather taxes to influential (and wealthy) local citizens. These people knew the location of taxable property, recorded it carefully, listed tax debt, and collected tax revenue with the backing of the Roman army. To say the least, the Jewish community despised their efforts as much as any country today living under "occupation" despises the work of collaborators.

"Sinners" is a generic term used in the Gospels by the Pharisees to describe those who have broken the law, those who are unclean, or those who have abandoned their full commitment to Jewish life. Any who embrace the culture of the Gentiles would no doubt qualify.

Luke 15 opens with Jesus receiving criticism for associating with such people. When the Pharisees argue that "this man welcomes sinners and eats with them," they are claiming that Jesus is at fault because he fully accepts people who have failed by every religious and social standard; this compromise of values implies that he has a deeply compromised faith. In other words, the accusation actually means, "Jesus is not righteous because he does not keep boundaries with the unrighteous."

AP Photo/Stuart Ramson

An orthodox Jewish gathering, New York

In response to these criticisms, Jesus tells three stories. The first two are deceptively simple; the third is perhaps his most complex. But in each case a similar argument is made: God delights in finding those living on the margin—those who are lost—and so likewise should those within the religious community.

But this is not all he wishes to say. In the third story commonly known as the parable of the prodigal son, Jesus carries the story further and asks a question that would at once stun and worry his critics. Note the symmetry in the three stories: something gets lost, a caregiver seeks to find it, and the community celebrates its return. The scale of the story narrows: a hundred sheep, ten coins, then two sons.

A Story about a Hundred Sheep

We must remember that Jesus' audience consists of Pharisees and scribes, men who viewed themselves as the custodians of right belief and right conduct. Now Jesus responds to their criticism with pedestrian stories whose sophistication might seem below them.

7. Radovan/www.BibleLandPictures.com

Sheep grazing in spring in the Judean hills

Suppose one of you has a hundred sheep and loses one of them. Doesn't he leave the ninety-nine in the open country and go after the lost sheep until he finds it? And when he finds it, he joyfully puts it on his shoulders and goes home. Then he calls his friends and neighbors together and says, "Rejoice with me; I have found my lost sheep." I tell you that in the same way there will be more rejoicing in heaven over one sinner who repents than over ninety-nine righteous persons who do not need to repent.

An Arab shepherd from 19th century Ottoman Palestine

In Jesus' day, shepherds were admired in Israel's literature and history (David and Moses were shepherds) but they were not esteemed by religious leaders. Not only did shepherds work in dangerous settings in the wilderness, but they were unable to keep the law there. To draw Jewish leaders into a story about sheep ("suppose *one of you* has one hundred sheep . . .") recalls the severe criticism of Ezekiel 34, where the prophet compares Israel's leaders with shepherds. How a shepherd takes care of his sheep tells everything about his devotion to them.

In this story Jesus' audience would make some natural assumptions. Such a flock reflects either a great deal of wealth or the collected animals of a community. This story probably implies the latter. And it is likely that this shepherd is not working alone. When one sheep is lost, he does not abandon the ninety-nine in the wilderness in order to find the lost one. Only a foolish shepherd does this. He sends the sheep back to the village *that awaits his return*. The shepherd knows the value of each sheep because he knows that all responsibility for them rests on his shoulders. To abandon ninety-nine sheep in the wild is to lose them immediately.

Locating a lost sheep alone, the shepherd assumes considerable risk. The Judean wilderness was a hostile place known for predators, robbers, and severe terrain. Yet when he finds the sheep, he hoists it on his shoulders, and climbs out. These are not level desert vistas. The Judean wilderness is rocky and irregular with deep valleys. To climb out alone is hard; to climb out with a fifty-pound sheep on your back is extreme. His village joins in the celebration of the lost sheep because they have known about its circumstances for some time. In village life, little happens that is private. The shepherd's absence and his adventures will be told over and over as people gather in the evening. When he returns, everyone gathers to "hear the story."

For Jesus, this presents a poignant picture of God's interest in those who are lost, those on the margin. God is no different than a skilled wilderness shepherd (see Ps. 23). And if any of his own sheep are lost, he will pursue them. This explains why Jesus is drawn to those on the margin of Judaism's social world. *They are the lost sheep of Israel*—and he seeks to find them.

A Story about Ten Coins

As if drawing Pharisees into a comparison with shepherds wasn't enough, Jesus now tells a story about a woman and her coins. Note how the parallels work: A shepherd (God) loses one sheep from a flock of a hundred and seeks until he finds it. In the Old Testament, the shepherd was the commonplace metaphor for God. Now *a woman* loses one coin out of ten. The numerical comparison narrows and the image of God as a searching woman must have been stunning.

> *Or suppose a woman has ten silver coins and loses one. Doesn't she light a lamp, sweep the house and search carefully until she finds it? And when she finds it, she calls her friends and neighbors together and says, "Rejoice with me; I have found my lost coin." In the same way, I tell you, there is rejoicing in the presence of the angels of God over one sinner who repents.*

Once more, important assumptions are in place. For a peasant people who grow their own food and make their own clothes, cash is a rare commodity. In fact, it is a security against the future in case of crisis. Women commonly kept coins on their bodies, often in a small bag, and these were their guarantee of sustenance in case of tragedy. Occasionally bags of coins were

Z. Radovan/www.BibleLandPictures.com

A silver coin from Tiberius, the era of Jesus.

hidden in the ceiling of the dwelling (which was made of wood, straw, and an exterior overlay of dried mud).

Here a woman lives in a small home without windows (glass windows are only in expensive public buildings in this period). Her floor is packed dirt. The corners are dark. And she knows how easy it is to lose a coin and not recover it. Such coins have been lost for centuries and today turn up in the spade work of archaeologists who disassemble such floors.

So she lights a lamp to illumine her work, she sweeps carefully every inch of her home, and when she finds the coin, she celebrates with her village. Again, great or tragic events are celebrated corporately (not privately). So with her friends, she rejoices and the telling of this story is the news of the day.

Jesus has now posed a second story-metaphor for the lost. A lost sheep has now become a lost coin. *When such valued items are found, is this not good reason to rejoice?* And naturally he hopes his audience will think of those lost coins that he has found among the sinners of Israel. "Outsiders" are not simply to be left outside; they should be brought "in" and restored.

A Story about Two Sons

We have seen a developing symmetry to the stories of Luke 15. A hundred sheep have become ten coins. Now this will narrow to two sons. In this final complex story, Jesus tells of one son who gets lost in the far country—and this is a duplication of the themes heard in the previous two stories. Something gets lost and its recovery is not only eagerly sought, but celebrated. But in this final story, Jesus adds "part two." And it is this part that takes his critics by surprise.

A Son Is Found: Part 1

This third story is perhaps Jesus' most complicated and intriguing. Contextual, cultural clues abound, and without them we miss its meaning.

> *There was a man who had two sons. The younger one said to his father, "Father, give me my share of the estate." So he divided his property between them.*
>
> *Not long after that, the younger son got together all he had, set off for a distant country and there squandered his wealth in wild living. After he had spent everything, there was a severe famine in that whole country, and he began to be in need. So he went and hired himself out to a citizen of that country, who sent him to his fields to feed pigs. He longed to fill his stomach with the pods that the pigs were eating, but no one gave him anything.*
>
> *When he came to his senses, he said, "How many of my father's hired servants have food to spare, and here I am starving to death! I will set out and go back to my father and say to him: Father, I have sinned against heaven and against you. I am no longer worthy to be called your son; make me like one of your hired servants." So he got up and went to his father.*
>
> *But while he was still a long way off, his father saw him and was filled with compassion for him; he ran to his son, threw his arms around him and kissed him.*

Z. Radovan/www.BibleLandPictures.com

A well-tended orchard, typical of a successful family

The son said to him, "Father, I have sinned against heaven and against you. I am no longer worthy to be called your son."

But the father said to his servants, "Quick! Bring the best robe and put it on him. Put a ring on his finger and sandals on his feet. Bring the fattened calf and kill it. Let's have a feast and celebrate. For this son of mine was dead and is alive again; he was lost and is found." So they began to celebrate.

Z. Radovan/www.BibleLandPictures.com

BARGAINING IN JERUSALEM

This younger son does not stray from the flock or get lost in a dirt floor; rather, he ruptures his relationship with his entire village. His request is a public insult to his father, and it is unprecedented in this culture. *No son requests his inheritance before his father's death*. It is the same as wishing your father were dead. The expected reflex is simple: such a son should be punished until he honors his father. But instead, this father *gives*.

A village father like this would not have cash assets to divide. He owns land, buildings, animals, and tools. For him to divide his estate and give disposable cash to his son, he must sell what he has to his village. And if he doesn't sell it, clearly his son will. And this starts the scandal spinning in town. *Why is he selling? What could his son have said? What if our sons get this idea in their heads?* Not only is the father's honor betrayed, but the entire village's values are offended. This village would be angry. This boy wants to cash in his sonship.

In this society land sales and personal property can take months of bargaining, all designed to measure the value of the item and preserve the honor of the seller. His boy sells fast and goes. He liquidates his estate. With cash in hand, the young man heads for the Gentile world ("distant country"), further offending the sensibilities of his Jewish village. This is Jacob trading his heritage for a pot of stew.

In the far country it is one thing to spend money on investment; it is quite another to spend money on entertainment. This young man does the latter in blind disregard for how vulnerable he is. In this world, life is sustained by the network of familial relationships. Your security is not in your bank account, but in your relationships. Arab society functions in precisely this manner. Lebanese living in war or Palestinians living under occupation—they survive by relying on extensive family networks both in the Middle East and around the world.

Then tragedy strikes. A famine sweeps through the region and crisis falls on every village. It is hard for Westerners to understand the threat of a genuine famine. Thanks to reservoirs and dams, even the modern Middle East rarely sees this. But in the ancient world, such famines were common. No water, no crops, no food—and desperate people will eat anything that is growing or living.

Our young man has no family, no help in the crisis. So he attaches himself to a Gentile citizen. This man no doubt sees him as a nuisance, recognizes his Jewish clothes and accent, and gives him a job he would surely refuse: feed pigs. Of course, a pig is an unclean animal to Jews and this man not only must feed them, but he *must eat the very food they eat*. In cultural terms, he has descended to the bottom. Luke 15:16 uses a Greek tense that implies he is asking, begging, for food, but in the famine there are no handouts.

He is awakened by memories of his father's estate. While he starves, his father's servants eat well. While he is alone, his family is no doubt protecting itself. So he makes a plan. He will return home, repent before his father, admit that he cannot be a son, and beg his father to make him a paid servant. He is not asking to be a household servant (Greek, *doulos*), who lives off the estate, eats from the kitchen, and benefits from the father's estate. He asks to be a *misthios*, that is, a "hired hand" (Greek *misthos* means wages). Perhaps with wages he can earn enough to repay the money he lost.

The son's return brings an unexpected scene. The son surely expects trouble. He has ruptured relationships with everyone: his father, his brother, his extended family, even the village. *Everyone is angry with him*. Yet, this is his only option

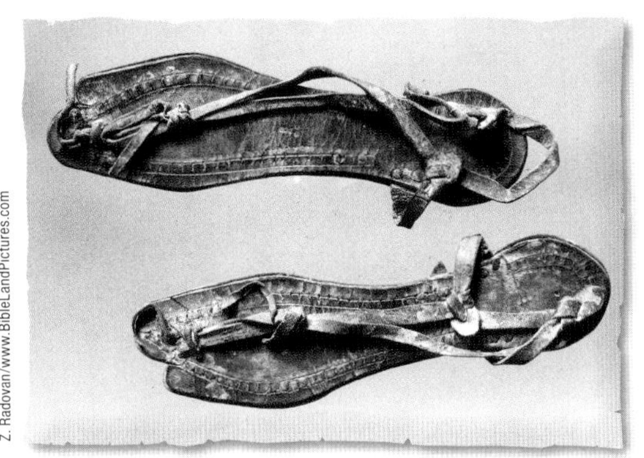

First century sandals discovered at the fortress of Masada near the Dead Sea

since in the far country he is dying.

As he approaches the village no doubt the many village children—every village has children playing in public—see him and a cry goes up. *That boy has returned! Let's see what happens to him!* A crowd forms, eyes cut to the horizon. And in the midst of the social chaos, the father runs, embraces him, and kisses him repeatedly. In this world, men of honor and prestige do not run. To do so is shaming. Yet at the turning point of the story, the young son's restoration costs his father his public honor.

Note that the son cannot produce his entire speech. There is no word of service. His game plan has been completely upended by unexpected charity, love, and grace. Quickly the father turns to one of his household servants (Greek *doulos*) and gives an order: dress him like a son (a family robe, a family ring) and give him sandals (only slaves are barefoot). With one order, the father publicly restores his son to the village and marches home with him. A son that was lost is now found.

A Samaritan celebration of Passover over 100 years ago

Recall that this is a famine and the father is a wealthy man. A calf—not a chicken or a lamb—is slaughtered *in famine* and the entire village is fed. This is a public restoration, a public forgiveness, a public celebration. The sheep has come home; the coin has returned.

A Son Is Lost: Part 2

These stories thus far parallel one another. Something is lost, it is found, great joy ensues. Now Jesus probes further. What about the ninety-nine and the nine? What are the attitudes of those who remain behind in the father's estate, who never get lost, and who view themselves as *righteous?*

> *Meanwhile, the older son was in the field. When he came near the house, he heard music and dancing. So he called one of the servants and asked him what was going on. "Your brother has come," he replied, "and your father has killed the fattened calf because he has him back safe and sound."*
>
> *The older brother became angry and refused to go in. So his father went out and pleaded with him. But he answered his father, "Look! All these years I've been slaving for you and never disobeyed your orders. Yet you never gave me even a young goat so I could celebrate with my friends. But when this son of yours who has squandered your property with prostitutes comes home, you kill the fattened calf for him!"*
>
> *"My son," the father said, "you are always with me, and everything I have is yours. But we had to celebrate and be glad, because this brother of yours was dead and is alive again; he was lost and is found."*

In ancient Middle Eastern culture the older son carries more responsibility than one life should have to bear. He inherits the lion's share of the estate (two-thirds), he protects the honor of the family name, he cares for his parents' welfare as they age, and while they live he is a man with great responsibility but little power. He has watched his brother deplete the estate and bring disrespect to his father. He has every right to be on his guard. What's left of the estate belongs to him—and a returning son who has behaved like his brother should not be trusted.

From the fields where he works—he is always working, never playing—he can hear the party. With so many hungry, famine-starved villagers in attendance, the noise carries easily. As the elder son, all parties would have been discussed with him—all costs weighed, even the slaughtered animal considered. But this is unannounced. So he calls to one of the boys on the street who knows all the day's news and the report emerges: "The family calf is on a spit! Your brother is back! Your father has thrown a party!"

Rembrandt's famous "Return of the Prodigal" (1669)

This infuriates him. Rather than discipline the wayward son, his father has shown generosity; rather than judgment, peace.

First sons have social responsibilities in Jesus' world. At family gatherings, they might serve as hosts and extend honor to all who arrive. This son is his father's pride (Arab men today name themselves after their first sons, e.g., Abu Nakhleh means *father of Nakhleh*) and his absence is noted. The whispers are predictable: What will the older son do? The father has been kind, but will his brother?

Again, the father experiences insult. A second time. From *outside* the estate, this son shames his father as well. "I will not enter" is a sentence that shoots through the party. This son's opponent is not his younger brother, but his father. But rather than standing inside his home with his guests waiting for his older son to arrive, this father does the unexpected: *he goes out.*

Luke 15:28–30 are perhaps the most important verses in this story. Here we listen in to the two complaints of the older son. Paraphrasing it restores its power. Without giving his father a respectful title (as culture demands), no doubt with the village listening in, he argues with him: "Look, you have not been generous with me. I worked like a slave for you in perfect righteousness but you credit little to me. Simply put, if you can do this—you owe me."

But his complaint runs deeper. "Besides, this calf infuriates me. I could have been consulted. You have been generous when you should have been strict. This boy has dishonored you and our family—and now by lacking righteousness yourself, you do the same." *These are the words of the Pharisees that no doubt Jesus hopes will ring in their ears.*

This public shaming parallels the public shaming of the younger son. When other fathers might have gone out to argue and fight, this father is filled once more with compassion. He calls out, "My son . . ."; in Greek the word is actually "child" (*teknon*). This man, this son now grown, is his child, a child whose behavior now perhaps echoes behavior of many years prior. *How often has self-proclaimed righteousness led to life-destroying pride?*

The father urges him to come in, reassuring him that his place has not been lost—that as first son he is still where he was, and that this is a fitting celebration. His brother is still his brother despite what has happened. He was lost, but now has been found.

In each of the other stories—the restoration of the sheep, the coin, and the younger son—leads to great happiness. Restoration means public celebration and cheer. Yet this second part of the final story, this tragic unfolding of a first son's anger, concludes without joy. The son is left in the estate courtyard, staring at his father, weighing his choices, wondering if it is time for him to take charge. We never know if he enters the party.

Faith and the Lost

The Pharisees' criticism of Jesus is simple: the righteous should set appropriate boundaries. By accepting sinners you accept their sin. But this is the premise Jesus refuses to acknowledge. Perhaps this is one of the features that distinguishes his entire ministry. Those who have fallen, who live on the margin, who know they are never good enough for religious society, who are deemed "lost"—these are the lost sheep Jesus seeks to find.

These parables are truly a reassurance to those lost sheep who have strayed. But they are also a warning—and this aspect of their message is generally missed. Men and women everywhere prefer to build communities that affirm their choices, that share their values, that keep out those who might bring unrighteousness to their neighborhoods.

Wheaton is well known for being a Chicago suburb with a fine Christian college and many churches. Crime is low, streets are clean, schools are tops, churches are full. Christian discussions about outreach are fine if we are talking about Chicago or Ghana. But it was a remarkable day when Prison Fellowship decided to purchase a home here, staff it professionally, and house a number of Christian ex-offenders. These were men who had served their time in prison, committed their lives to Christ, passed screening tests, and now wanted to live among us. *The uproar was astonishing.* To put this story in first-century terms, *these were the unrighteous and they had no place here.* Fortunately, the case against Prison Fellowship failed, their home has remained, and few think about it anymore.

Lost sons sometimes have difficulty coming home because of their older brothers. Lost sheep sometimes choose to be lost because of the judgments made within the church. Jesus preferred the margins, the wilderness, the places where people were lost. Those who enjoyed self-congratulatory lives likely took less interest in him.

ביתרבי אבון

Chapter 7

THE FOOLISH BUILDER

Luke 12:13–21

FEW SCENES are as timeless or cross-cultural as the division of property following the death of a parent or grandparent. I have seen this in my family (*Who is getting that sterling silver?*) and many others. The modern Middle Eastern world is no exception to such tensions. Property, particularly in the form of land, represents a family's legacy. To own a part of it is not merely about money and value, it is about owning the future, having a place, being honored by others. When Psalm 133:1 describes "how good and pleasant it is when brothers live together in unity" (NIV), it may have this backdrop in mind. A great tragedy befalls a family when brothers (or sisters) exhaust their friendships over the spoils recorded in a will.

In the villages of Judea and Galilee, rabbis were generally called on to resolve civil disputes such as those involving inheritance. Their role was not merely leadership and instruction within the village community, but the administration of justice. In Matthew 23:23 Jesus reminds the Pharisees that the pursuit of such justice is precisely what they should do. In Luke 18:3 Jesus tells another story about a woman who cries outside the local court begging for "justice

A RURAL HOUSE
Z.Radovan/www.BiblelandPictures.com

against my adversary." We can assume that this is a civil matter, likely about inheritance, and in her case her welfare and survival depend on the outcome.

Even though Jesus is not formally a rabbi, his reputation has preceded him. In a Galilee village he is approached to be a family arbiter — and then he tells a story to help his listeners see their problem with common sense graced by how God views these matters.

Todd Bolen/www.BiblePlaces.com

A RABBI CELEBRATES SUKKOT IN JERUSALEM

JESUS THE ARBITER

In Luke's gospel, Jesus has just completed his astoundingly popular ministry in Galilee (Luke 4:14 – 9:51). His fame is widely known from such great events as the healing of a centurion's slave, the raising of a synagogue leader's daughter, and the feeding of the five thousand. Even his disciples have seen him transfigured on a mountain. Therefore at 9:51 he decides to begin a journey to Jerusalem. As he moves south through Galilee, many recognize him thanks in no small part to his sending seventy disciples ahead to announce his coming (10:1). Luke 12:1 describes "a crowd of many thousands" who gather "so that they are trampling on one another." This is almost the peak of his public popularity.

It is no surprise that as Jesus enters one village he is approached to mediate a family quarrel (Luke 12:13 – 14). A man with his fame would certainly be able to settle a dispute and all arguing parties would be silenced. So "someone in the crowd said to him, 'Teacher, tell my brother to divide the inheritance with me.' Jesus replied, 'Man, who appointed me a judge or an arbiter between you [plural]?' "

The Greek address "teacher" (*didaskalos*) disguises the

Hebrew title *rabbi*. This is both a form of respect (all respectful speech should begin with a title in this culture) and an appeal to Jesus' authority now popularly recognized. But note carefully how the request is formed. This is not a plea for true mediation. The man has not said, "Our father has died and we need to divide his estate; please help us." This is a man who has made up his mind, a man who is looking for an authoritative voice that will give an order to his brother. Perhaps he is a second son and his brother has claimed the whole of the estate improperly. In truth, this inheritance has come at a steep cost: two brothers are now estranged and the losing brother is demanding his share. And it is likely the case that land (our "inheritance") is at question.

Jesus' response is unexpected. He likewise titles his response ("Man," Greek, *anthrope*), and with it conveys an important disapproving tone. He does not like what he sees. This is not about impartial mediation; it is a demand to take sides. Therefore Jesus rejects the role placed before him. He refuses to make a judgment—and he refuses to be an "arbiter" or *divider* (Greek, *meristes*).

Z. Radovan/www.BibleLandPictures.com

A CAREFULLY MEASURED ORCHARD NEAR BETHLEHEM

The word *meristes* is rare in the New Testament. In Greek *meris* (also *meros*) is a "part" (Luke 11:36; Acts 16:12) or a portion (Acts 8:21). *Merismos* is a division or a distribution of something large (Heb. 4:12). A *meristes* is someone who makes such divisions. Jesus will not stand between these two men and make the division of their property. They need to realize that there is something more valuable here than property. Reconciliation, not division, should be their interest. In one sense, Jesus will become a judge *over them*, not *between them*.

A Wisdom Saying

The Jewish tradition was rich with sayings of "wisdom." These were proverbial truths presented in the abstract time-tested ideas that were preserved for posterity. The Old Testament book of Proverbs contains one such collection—and there were many more. Therefore Jesus begins his judgment of the situation with a proverb of his own: "Then he said to them, 'Watch out! Be on your guard against all kinds of greed; life does not consist in an abundance of possessions.' "

The warning here is often translated as if greed or coveting were the problem. This is merely a symptom. Both Jewish and Hellenistic writers from this era decried the corrupting influence of greed. For many it was the root of most evil. The deeper problem here is how one will view life. In Jesus' world possessing land (or wealth) was closely related to gaining social prestige and honor. Thus by gaining property, this man is hoping that the property will aid him in gaining social status. This is what Jesus means by "life." Possessions are not the measure of the good life. He is trying to move beyond the estate squabble and probe what drives it. We will see this again when Jesus attaches another wisdom saying echoing the same theme in the following short story.

The Rich Fool

Judaism was rich with reflection on the dilemma of wealth and death. Psalm 49:16–20 warns that the pursuit of wealth is fleeting. Ecclesiastes 2:1–11 describes the futility of building expansive estates (such as Solomon's) and keeping it for eternity (in the Apocrypha, see also Sir. 11). Such literature also enjoys telling about the contrasts between the fool and the wise

Todd Bolen/www.BiblePlaces.com

Ancient storehouses excavated in Beersheba, Israel

person. This story describes the fate of a wealthy man whose pursuits *in this life* have been richly rewarded. And we learn that in the end, he is a fool.

> *And [Jesus] told them this parable: "The ground of a certain rich man yielded an abundant harvest. He thought to himself, 'What shall I do? I have no place to store my crops.'*
>
> *"Then he said, 'This is what I'll do. I will tear down my barns and build bigger ones, and there I will store my surplus grain. And I'll say to myself, "You have plenty of grain laid up for many years. Take life easy; eat, drink and be merry."' "*

Jesus lived in a world where the successes of farming were dependent on many things beyond a person's control. Expensive fertilizers, hybrid seed, and mechanized farming were unavailable to increase a crop yield. Much simply depended on rain—and this was in God's hands. This story, therefore, implies that these crops are a gift—note that the "ground" produced this crop—and it suggests something the farmer cannot yet imagine: God has been responsible for his wealth.

Because of a failure to recognize the source of his farming success, this rich man's only consideration is how to store these surpluses. "He thought to himself" builds a picture of a man struggling with a happy dilemma. He has more money than he can spend, more cars than he can drive, more food than he can eat. His facilities will not contain the surplus.

Moreover, this farmer does not weigh his problem within the community of his village as one would expect. This is a solitary man counting his wealth alone, enjoying the isolation that so often prosperity provides. Throughout Luke's gospel this solitary self-talk is characteristic of those who are in error or deceived (Luke 5:21–22; 6:8; 9:46–47). Note how he refers to these as "my crops." This is about his achievement, his prosperity. There is not hint of thanks to God. Ecclesiastes 5:10 may have offered him advice: "Those who love money never have enough; those who love wealth are never satisfied with their income. This too is meaningless."

However, the farmer's reflex to store up surpluses is understandable given the fragile condition of life in the Middle East. Famines were common (we know from various sources of about a dozen famines in the New Testament period), and farming abundance was something to be treasured. But there may be another motive. If his crops are abundant, so are the others around him, and the market value of this produce is certainly low. Rather than sell now, he chooses to hold—and bring these things to market in a poor year, thus yielding even sharper profits.

The deepest problem within the farmer's life is finally uncovered in Luke 12:19: "And I'll say to myself, 'You have plenty of grain laid up for many years. Take life easy; eat, drink and be merry.' " Older translations show the literal Greek form of the pronouncement, "I will say to my soul, 'Soul. . . .' " The Greek word *psyche* ("soul") can refer to "myself," but it also can represent the Hebrew word *nephesh*, meaning the totality of a person's life. The

Todd Bolen/www.BiblePlaces.com

Grape harvest in Wadi Biyyar, Palestine

Todd Bolen/www.BiblePlaces.com

Grape harvest near Dor, Israel

farmer is engaging in self-conversation that does not lead to self-reflection. He is not "thinking critically"; he is engaged in a self-congratulatory assessment of his world. *His life has turned out just as he wanted it to.*

One senses that his life has made him proud. He feels his efforts have made him self-sufficient, autonomous, invulnerable—he is holding the winning investment portfolio and a winning strategy for life. He couldn't be happier.

Many scholars point out a delicate Greek wordplay inside the story. In 12:16 we learned that the man's life "brought forth plentifully" (*euphoreo*); now in verse 19 he says, "Enjoy yourself" (*euphraino*). These words are related. In Greek *phoreo* refers to bearing fruit; adding *eu* (*euphoreo*) intensifies it, so that it means "to prosper richly." Thus the term can refer to joy, and happiness (*euphrosyne* is what you may experience at a festival, abundant happiness, as in the English word *euphoria*). Thus the connection here is made: a fruitful yield leads to a fruitful life; a prosperous farm means a prosperous soul; riches will give you the rich life.

At this point in the story Jesus could have ended with a crisp warning about wealth and how it can seduce our souls and induce us to lose faith in God. The Jewish world was filled with these sorts of warnings. A detour through the first few chapters of Ecclesiastes might do it. But this is not how Jesus' stories work. Suddenly he forces the story into a sharp turn when God intervenes in the deceived farmer's life. "But God said to him, 'You fool! This very night your life will be demanded from you. Then who will get what you have prepared for yourself?' "

Greed and foolishness are often linked in Jewish moral teaching. Fools deny the ultimate lordship of God and repudiate his teaching (Prov. 14:1). And in their pursuit of happiness their pursuit of money is seen as reckless. "One becomes rich through diligence and self-denial ... [but] he does not know how long it will be until he leaves them to others and dies" (Sir. 11:18–19).

In Jesus' parable suddenly God intervenes with a shock, "You fool!" Greek sometimes negates a word with a preceding "*a*," much like we do in English (*symmetry*, *asymmetry*). And one potent term for foolishness is *aphron*, the very term used here. The man, in fact, lacks the very thing he thought he possessed. He is not *euphron* but *aphron*; he is not living with abundance but in emptiness. He is not rich but bankrupt. He is impoverished.

He dies. Immediately. There is no time to make plans, no time to review the records from his last investments, no more enjoyment of this world. *This very night* God will take back what he had given to him: his life. The expression used here ("demanded") is used in Greek for repayment of a loan or stolen property. His life has been on loan—a gift from God—and now its use is finished. And the newly built barns with their contents? They are lost. Ironically, he will never know what happens to the estate fights that follow his death. His quest for security and comfort has now led to a dead end. *God is the ultimate arbiter of life and property.*

Library of Congress, LC-matpc-06417/www.LifeintheHolyLand.com

Poor peasants in 19th century Jerusalem

A Final Wisdom Saying

The force of the final words from Jesus crystallizes the assertion of the story. He ends with a crisp proverbial saying: "This is how it will be with those who store up things for themselves but are not rich toward God."

The saying enjoys a symmetry that is lost in English. A translation that strains English but retains the sense of the original might look like this: "Thus [it will be for] (1) those storing up for themselves and (2) those not making riches for God." At issue is not whether a person is "rich" toward God (the usual translation) but whether he or she is contributing to a wealth valued by God. It is not a status but a series of choices and activities. People choose: either to enrich themselves or to enrich their relationship with God.

The Greek term for "storing up" is related to the Greek word for "treasure" (*thesauros*; see Matt. 6:21). This man is *treasuring* life in the sense that he is hoarding it, hiding it, controlling its resources, putting it in treasure boxes. The option he has missed has to do with recognizing not only that God has given him all he has—including his life—and, therefore, he has an obligation to honor God for what he has done.

Z. Radovan/www.BibleLandPictures.com

A HORDE OF TYREAN SILVER SHEKELS

Faith and the Parable

Frequently the stories of Jesus are followed by some response in the audience. But in this case the man in dispute with his brother is silent. *This is not the answer he is looking for.* His mind is on accumulation and self-interest. He has not approached Jesus looking for a moral exhortation or a reminder about his own mortality. Nevertheless this is the heart of Jesus' warning. Our use of the things of this world is less about ownership and chiefly about stewardship. The valuation of our investments is measured by God in a manner that may not be recognized on earth. "This very night your life will be demanded from you" is a reminder that checks our impulses to hoard and be selfish.

My first reminder of this truth came to me a few years ago in the life of an old seminary friend named John Bennett. John was an incredibly talented man whose energies surpassed any of us. When he married my wife's college roommate, the four of us became good friends. I followed a life into academics, John built mission agencies and traveled the world. (ACMC, The

Association of Church Mission Agencies, was begun by him.) Then one night at age forty-seven—during dinner—John felt discomfort in his chest. He reassured his two children from the back door of the ambulance before they drove off with sirens blaring. But within sixty minutes, John was with the Lord. "This very night your life will be demanded from you." John's rich legacy is a network of ministries that support mission work on almost every continent.

I think of another friend here in Chicago. He is one of my heroes. Few know it but he is tremendously wealthy from a bricklaying business he built up over the many good years of his life. Indeed, he could have built great "riches for himself," but instead he has poured countless dollars into a mission school in Ecuador and into an urban ministry in one of Chicago's poorest and most violent neighborhoods. Recently he rounded up all of his children and grandchildren and flew all of them down to Ecuador for a "vacation." But his agenda became clear; they would work serving others, catch his vision for this country, and commit themselves to making sure his estate would continue to help such needs. This is a man of inspiring faith whose legacy of generosity—not hoarding—will inspire his two sons and his grandchildren to do the same.

Ancient Context, Ancient Faith

The Bible and the Land

Gary M. Burge

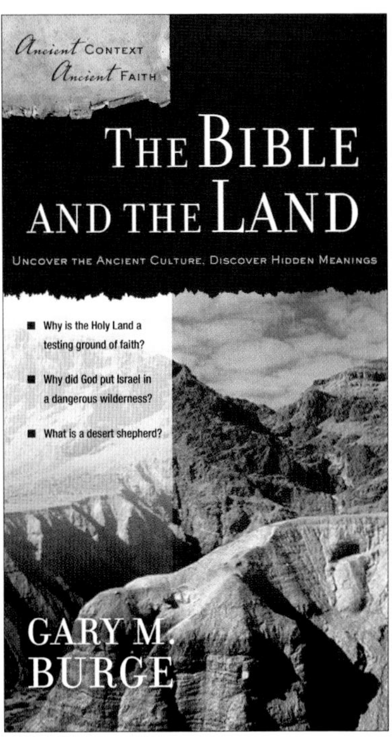

As the early church moved away from the original cultural setting of the Bible and found its home in the west, Christians lost touch with the ancient world of the Bible. Cultural habits, the particulars of landscape, even the biblical languages soon were unknown. And the cost was enormous: Christians began reading the Bible as foreigners and missing the original images and ideas that shaped a biblical worldview.

The Bible and the Land, by New Testament scholar Gary M. Burge, launches a multivolume series that explores how the culture of the biblical world is presupposed in story after story of the Bible. Using cultural anthropology, ancient literary sources, and a selective use of modern Middle Eastern culture, Burge reopens the ancient biblical story and urges us to look at them through new lenses. He explores primary motifs from the biblical landscape—geography, water, rock, bread, etc.—and applies them to vital stories from the Bible.

Each volume in the *Ancient Context, Ancient Faith* series is full color, rich with photographs, and in a travel size for convenient Bible study anywhere you go.

Softcover: 978-0-310-28044-6

Share Your Thoughts

With the Author: Your comments will be forwarded to the author when you send them to *zauthor@zondervan.com.*

With Zondervan: Submit your review of this book by writing to *zreview@zondervan.com.*

Free Online Resources at

www.zondervan.com

Zondervan AuthorTracker: Be notified whenever your favorite authors publish new books, go on tour, or post an update about what's happening in their lives.

Daily Bible Verses and Devotions: Enrich your life with daily Bible verses or devotions that help you start every morning focused on God.

Free Email Publications: Sign up for newsletters on fiction, Christian living, church ministry, parenting, and more.

Zondervan Bible Search: Find and compare Bible passages in a variety of translations at www.zondervanbiblesearch.com.

Other Benefits: Register yourself to receive online benefits like coupons and special offers, or to participate in research.